Quilts, BABY!

20 Cuddly Designs to Piece, Patch & Embroider

Linda Kopp

LARK BOOKS
A Division of Sterling Publishing Co., Inc.
New York / London

technical editor
Susan Huxley

art director
Kathleen Holmes

editorial assistance
Amanda Carestio

illustrators
Susan McBride
& Orrin Lundgren

photographer
Keith Wright

cover designer
Susan McBride

editorial interns
Jacob Biba
& Courtney Metz

Library of Congress Cataloging-in-Publication Data

Kopp, Linda, 1960-

Quilts, baby! : 20 cuddly designs to piece, patch & embroider / Linda Kopp.—1st ed.

p. cm.

Includes index.

ISBN 978-1-60059-330-7 (pb-pbk. with flaps : alk. paper)

1. Patchwork—Patterns. 2. Embroidery—Patterns. 3. Children's quilts. I. Title.

TT835.K6663 2009

746.46'041—dc22

2008033514

10 9 8 7 6 5 4 3 2 1

First Edition

Published by Lark Books, A Division of Sterling Publishing Co., Inc.
387 Park Avenue South, New York, NY 10016

© 2009, Lark Books

Distributed in Canada by Sterling Publishing, c/o Canadian Manda Group, 165 Dufferin Street, Toronto, Ontario, Canada M6K 3H6

Distributed in the United Kingdom by GMC Distribution Services, Castle Place, 166 High Street, Lewes, East Sussex, England BN7 1XU

Distributed in Australia by Capricorn Link (Australia) Pty Ltd., P.O. Box 704, Windsor, NSW 2756 Australia

The written instructions, photographs, designs, patterns, and projects in this volume are intended for the personal use of the reader and may be reproduced for that purpose only. Any other use, especially commercial use, is forbidden under law without written permission of the copyright holder.

Every effort has been made to ensure that all the information in this book is accurate. However, due to differing conditions, tools, and individual skills, the publisher cannot be responsible for any injuries, losses, and other damages that may result from the use of the information in this book.

If you have questions or comments about this book, please contact:

Lark Books
67 Broadway
Asheville, NC 28801
828-253-0467

Manufactured in China

ISBN 13: 978-1-60059-330-7

For information about custom editions, special sales, premium and corporate purchases, please contact Sterling Special Sales Department at 800-805-5489 or specialsales@sterlingpub.com.

Quilts, BABY!

Contents

Rock-a-bye, baby!

When you think of a baby quilt, what comes to mind: happy little rainbows, dancing cherubs, smiling clowns—all rendered in pastels? Perhaps plump cavorting puppies and simpering kittens with a ghastly eye-to-face ratio? Or heaven forbid, the dreaded licensed cartoon character? Frankly, we think all of those are kind of scary, especially the clowns. And we feel the baby in your life deserves something cooler… way cooler.

We've assembled what we're quite sure is the hippest collection of baby quilts around: no pastel borders, no precious moments, and no sugary stuff. But let there be no mistake: these quilts definitely have the "awww" factor. Who for instance, could resist dogs in red pumps (page 30), a herd of sea horses (page 79), or 3-D monkeys (page 71)? While many of these quilts include fresh, modern elements, we haven't gone forth without a nod to traditional quilts. Stair-Crazy (page 96) offers a fresh, indie take on a traditional stair-step design while All Lined Up (page 122) puts an organic, wonderfully imperfect spin on the time-proven log cabin.

A little iffy with the sewing machine? Baby quilts make the perfect starter projects for new quilters, but they're also the ideal mini-canvas for seasoned pros who want to add oodles of detail to their creations. If you're new to quilting or just need a refresher on some of the techniques, you'll find in-depth instructions in the Basics section, in many cases accompanied with step-by-step illustrations.

We realize quilting is a methodical, time-honored tradition, but we also recognize that not everyone has vast amounts of leisure time. So we challenged the designers to come up with knock-your-socks-off quilts that could be made pretty much in a weekend. That being said, many of the quilts feature clever, bold designs, and shortcuts, snippets, and tidbits that will help speed you on your way and make the most of your time. Variation ideas provide the perfect inspiration for customizing the designs to your tastes (wc mcan baby's tastes, of course) or for creating a quilt design that's all your own imagining.

A handmade quilt is the perfect gift for a baby. It's personal and will be used and cherished long after most other gifts are outgrown. There's really nothing quite like being wrapped up in or tucked beneath a handmade quilt, especially when that quilt is über chic!

The Basics

Baby quilts just plain rock, and let us count the ways. Don't want to take out a loan to pay for quilting materials? Did baby arrive before you had time to make that matching crocheted blanket, onesie, and diaper bag set you were planning? Baby quilts to the rescue! You can create most of these stellar quilts with just a few basic sewing supplies and a couple of days, perfect for that baby shower next weekend that you forgot about (oopsy!). First things first, though: let's talk quilting basics.

La Quilt Sandwich

There's really nothing mysterious about the quilting process, especially when you break it down into parts (see figure 1). Think of your quilt as a sandwich (mmmm…) made of the quilt top, the batting, and the backing.

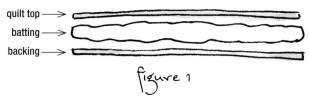

quilt top →
batting →
backing →

figure 1

The quilt top is what most people envision when they think "quilt." Whether it's pieced (small pieces or scraps of fabric sewn together into a larger design), appliquéd (fabric shapes stitched onto the quilt top fabric), or embroidered (shapes, designs, and even text created using various decorative stitches), the quilt top is the most visual part of the quilt design. Consequently, you'll want to spend the most time and creativity on your quilt top, especially if you plan on showing off your creation, which we highly encourage.

Batting is the layer of fabric stuffing that ensures your quilt is warm and cozy. There are a variety of batting materials out there to choose from, each with different qualities as well as levels of thickness (we'll talk more about batting later).

The backing is essentially the underside of the quilt. Although largely outshined by the quilt top (alack and alas), you can make your backing as plain or decorative as you like. You can use a complementary fabric to those featured on the quilt top, sew together larger blocks of fabric for a little bit of interest, or create a whole other design for a reversible quilt, like Good Night, Moon, Good Morning, Sun (page 55); the choice is yours.

When you're ready to assemble your quilt, you'll simply stack these layers one on top of the other and quilt—or stitch—them together. Bada-boom, bada-bing!

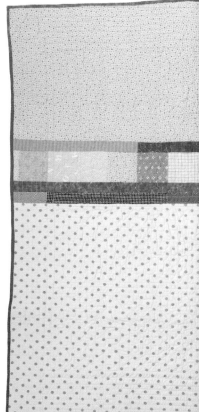

The Ingredients

If you need an excuse to do a tiny bit of shopping, look no further. You'll need to gather a few assorted materials and tools before you sit down to make your masterpiece.

FABRIC

If you spent more time at a fabric store than cleaning your house last month, you're in good company. Picking out fabrics is super fun, and it's an easy way to put your creative stamp on a project. Whether paisley prints, snappy stripes, or hand-dyed solids are your poison (and you don't have to pick just one), the options are endless. And they don't stop at the fabric store: try using thrift store finds—such as curtains, sheets, or pillowcases—or family "heirlooms" (untossable concert or vacation t-shirts, much-loved childhood bed sheets, and the like).

If you're new to sewing, it might be a good idea to stick to simple cotton since it's easier to work with and less likely to pucker. Steer toward mid-weight cottons over thinner cottons; mid-weight will hold up much better over time. If

Pleasantly Plump Quarters

Okay, they're called fat quarters and, thank you very much, they're just the right size. Sold individually at fabric stores and mildly addictive, fat quarters are handy when you need just a little bit of many different fabrics. They measure 18 by 22 inches (45.7 x 55.9 cm), meaning they're essentially a quarter yard cut in half.

you've fallen hard for a particular fabric, go ahead and buy a little extra since sometimes accidents do happen. In most cases, you'll need to prewash your fabric to avoid any later color bleeding or shrinkage snafus.

BATTING

Although essentially utilitarian in nature, batting is the "meat" (or "veggie burger" if you prefer) of your quilting sandwich. Low-loft batting, or thinner batting, is a great choice for a quilt with a lot of detail. This thickness is perfect for your sewing machine and most climates. High-loft batting—thicker stuff like that in a comforter—will be warmer and puffier. However, in all that lofty luxury, you might lose some of the quilt's definition, especially any hand-stitched elements.

Besides thickness, batting is available in a variety of materials from cotton to blends to polyester. Since your quilt is likely for a wee one, you might want to pick batting that's hypoallergenic and/or organic. You should also think about how the quilt will eventually be washed: polyester and polyester blends can usually survive a gentle machine wash and tumble dry, while cotton batting cannot. For the most flexibility, pick a batting that is fairly stable and strongly woven, meaning it won't move, shift, or bunch with use.

You can buy batting at most fabric stores. It's available in a variety of widths right off the bolt, like fabric, or in precut sizes, including an ultra-handy crib size that measures

9

45 x 60 inches (114.3 x 152.4 cm). In general, follow the pattern instructions for the type and quantity of batting to purchase. Keep in mind that your batting will need to be a few inches longer and wider than your quilt top, so shop accordingly. If you can't find batting that's exactly as wide or as long as your quilt, don't sweat it. Using a simple zigzag stitch along the edges, you can easily join pieces of batting to make the size you need.

THREAD

In most cases, your average all-purpose thread, usually a cotton/polyester blend, will do just fine. Many of the quilts in this book call for quilting thread, which is slightly finer and stronger than all-purpose thread. If you want your quilting stitches to blend in with the background, pick a color that matches your main fabrics or, as with Good Night Moon, Good Morning, Sun (page 55), you might even try a clear nylon thread. If, however, the quilting stitches are an important design element, make them stand out by selecting thread of bold, contrasting color.

Manic for Organic?

Want baby to start off green? There are plenty of ways to increase the "green" factor of your baby quilt. Check out the Web or your local fabric store for organic fabric, wool, and batting that are good for baby and the environment. Up-cycling is another easy way to go green. Try incorporating reused clothing, remnants, and pieces of other quilts—or even old pantyhose, as one designer's grandmother used for batting—into your project.

SCISSORS OR ROTARY CUTTING SYSTEM

You won't get very far in quilting without a fabulous pair of scissors, and it's best to have a pair dedicated just for this purpose (no Fido-hair-trimming or cardboard-fort-making allowed). To make life easier, you might also think about investing in a rotary cutting system, perfect for cutting strips and blocks of fabric often used in quilting. The system includes a rotary cutter (think pizza cutter, but avoid the temptation!), a measured and grid-lined mat, and a clear, thick plastic ruler with grid lines and measurements. All you do is line up your fabric on the grid, place the ruler where you'd like to cut, and roll the cutter along the ruler's edge. The cutter can easily slice through a couple of layers of folded or stacked fabrics, cutting your time in half and, in some instances, making your cuts more accurate.

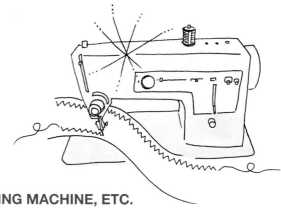

SEWING MACHINE, ETC.

A definitive benefit of the modern age, a sewing machine is a must if you want to complete your quilt quickly, especially since the arrival of your quilt's intended recipient can be a little hard to predict. Any standard sewing machine will suffice for most of the projects in this book, but machines with special stitching capabilities (like satin, zigzag, or blanket stitches) can help you fake those hand-stitched details like a pro.

Quilting Tool Kit

- ○ Scissors and a rotary cutting system
- ○ Needles for hand sewing
- ○ Safety or basting pins
- ○ Fabric chalk, marker, or pencil
- ○ Iron and ironing board
- ○ Sewing machine (optional)
- ○ Appliqué (or other straight) pins
- ○ Tape measure

NEEDLES FOR HAND SEWING

Try as you might, you'll probably have to do a teensy amount of hand stitching before your quilt is ready for battle. Have a few all-purpose sewing needles (a.k.a. sharps) on hand for times when precision work is needed.

QUILTING FRAME

Nothing brings to mind quilting days of yore like ye olde quilting frame. While certainly not necessary, a frame is handy for making sure your quilt top, batting, and backing are flat before you start stitching the layers together. If you're handy with a saw and hammer, it's easy to find free instructions to make a quilting frame online, at a local fabric shop, or in back issues of quilting magazines at the library. For flattening small areas, an embroidery hoop will work nicely, especially the kind with a screw that tightens the outer loop.

" People have been doing this for hundreds of years. You can, too. Just start—it's only fabric and thread. **"**
— Erin Harris

see my quilt on page 102

OTHER SUPPLIES

You probably already own the rest of the supplies you'll need to create the projects in this book: a collection of safety or curved basting pins (pins with a bend in the poker arm for reaching through thick quilt layers), appliqué pins (often with a flower-shaped head), quilting pins, a ruler, a fabric marker (either chalk or water-soluble ink), a tape measure, and an iron and ironing board.

APPLIQUÉ AND EMBROIDERY SUPPLIES & TOOLS

If you're planning on doing any amount of appliqué or embroidery on your quilts, you'll need a few extra supplies and tools. All you really need for either technique is fabric, a needle, and thread, but a few additional items will make your life much easier.

While hand appliqué is certainly a noble pursuit, do yourself a favor and get some fusible web. Cheap and easy to use, fusible web is attached to the back side of the fabric before the appliqué design is cut out, essentially creating an iron-on appliqué shape. Although an unlikely ally, freezer paper deserves a definite spot in your supply closet, making those tiny appliqué seam allowances a breeze to master.

For embroidery designs, you'll need to gather the usual suspects: embroidery needles (a standard embroidery needle is fine for most materials), embroidery floss or perle cotton, and an embroidery hoop. Having graphite paper and a pencil on hand can make planning and transferring embroidery designs a snap.

Getting Started

Sure, you're excited, but you've still got a few more steps before the quilting extravaganza can commence. A little planning and prep work can help you make the most of your fabric, your time, and this book. Once this work is done, it's time to get the show on the road.

PLANNING

The designs in this book are meant to supply inspiration. You can use the designs as they are presented, make small adjustments to suit your taste, or use one of these quilts as a springboard for your own imaginative design. Whatever your approach may be, it's best to plan it out well in advance. Use a notepad to jot down a list of things that you'll have to go to the fabric store for, to scribble out yardage calculations or adjustments (yuck!), and to draw the design for your next quilt when inspiration strikes (probably soon!).

SIZING THINGS UP

Unless they're intended to be art quilts or wall hangings, most of the quilts in this book measure between 36 x 48 inches (91.4 x 121.9 cm) and 48 x 60 inches (121.9 x 152.4 cm) to fit the standard crib size, which is 28 inches (71.1 cm) wide by 52 inches (132.1 cm) long. A rectangle seems like the most obvious choice, but you can make your quilt any size or shape—even round, like Peekaboo on page 66. A larger quilt might make sense if the babushka is a little older, whereas a smaller quilt might be better if you're using it as a throw or for traveling purposes, where it will no doubt (hint, hint) have a larger pool of potential admirers. Any of the quilts in this book can be made larger or smaller; just enlarge the templates and measurements as you see fit.

USING QUILTING CHARTS AND TEMPLATES

Along with the absolutely splendid designs in this book, you'll find a number of highly useful cutting charts and whole quilt templates as well as appliqué and embroidery patterns. Cutting charts are just that: charts that tell you how big or small to cut your various fabrics. You'll find them right with the quilt instructions along with the whole quilt templates—which serve as patterns for cutting your fabric. Appliqué and embroidery patterns are located in the back of the book.

To use the whole quilt templates and the appliqué and embroidery patterns, enlarge what you need on a photocopier to the recommended percentage. Then for whole quilt templates or appliqué patterns, cut out the paper piece (or pieces) and trace the shapes onto fabric with a fabric marker, or pin the template (right side up) to the fabric (also right side up) to use as a guide while you cut. For embroidery patterns, transfer the design lines (see page 18) to your fabric for easy, follow-the-lines stitching.

CUTTING

Before you do anything else, make sure you wash your fabrics first, using the same settings that will be used when laundering the finished quilt. If your fabric gets super

> **"**My advice to all people doing any creative project is to chill out! Put your rulers away and have some fun. It's nice to follow instructions for a while, until you get the hang of it, but then it's time to throw caution to the wind and have a go all by yourself.**"**
> —Carly Schwerdt
> see my quilt on page 66

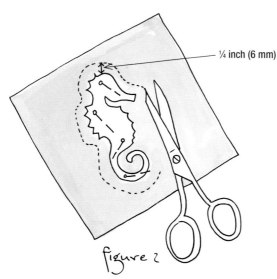

figure 2

wrinkly in the wash, give it a quick pressing before you continue working. Then, and only then, should you begin cutting (seriously, we have spies).

Whether you're using a ruler or templates to cut your fabric, you'll need to add about ¼ inch (6 mm) to each edge to accommodate the seam allowance (see figure 2), unless the instructions tell you not to or your appliqué shapes will not be turned under (in which case you can cut right next to the template). The instructions for each project tell you what you should do, so don't worry. You can cut all your pieces before you start or cut them along the way as needed; it's best to keep your pieces organized and even labeled if you're working with a complicated pattern.

Putting Things Together

You've embraced the sandwich concept, you've prepped and cut your fabrics, and you've got a master plan. You, my friend, are ready for action.

SEWING

Pheww…finally, on to the sewing! For all sewing tasks, you'll need to be mindful of the seam allowance—the distance between the seam and the cut edge of the fabric. Most of these sewing-specific tasks involve the same process: pinning fabric pieces together with right sides facing, stitching along one edge, and then ironing the seams open or to one side. The position of the seam allowances, whether together on one side of the seam or pressed open, is important because the seam allowances do add bulk and stability. Most of the project instructions will tell you what to do. When this guidance isn't included, you can do what seems right for your quilt. The rules change a bit when it comes to appliqué and embroidery, but the basic sewing principles and tools are essentially the same.

The seam allowances will be listed in each project, although ¼ inch (6 mm) is pretty standard. If you're using a sewing machine, use the measurement lines on the throat plate as a guide while you feed the fabric along, as shown in figure 3. But don't worry: no rocket science is necessary!

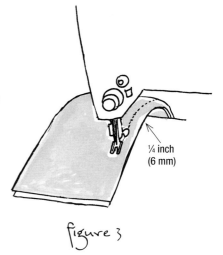

figure 3

Piecing

While some quilts in this book only involve appliqué or embroidery (in which the design elements are added directly on top of the quilt top), others involve some amount of piecing, a process used in most traditional quilts. During the piecing process, individual fabric pieces (hence the name) of the quilt top are sewn together into small units. The small units are then sewn together into larger units that are then sewn together again (depending on the quilt) to create the overall quilt design.

If you have an abundance of free time on your hands, or don't have access to a sewing machine, piecing by hand can be quite a satisfying endeavor, and some people find hand stitching to be relaxing. For the rest of us, a sewing machine is best, and, with a few shortcuts, the piecing process will fly by. Either way, the steps are quite simple.

Cutting Corners

Chain Gang

Got a whole stack of piecing to do? Feed them through your sewing machine one right after another with just a little space between them. In the end, you'll have a length of pieces that you can cut apart and use individually.

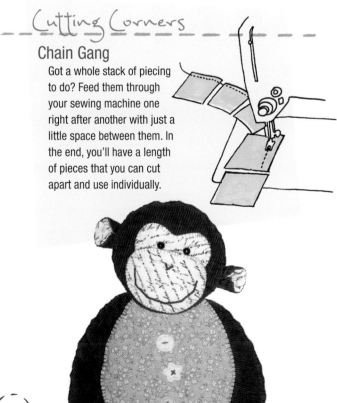

1. Lay two pieces of fabric together with right sides facing.

2. Pin the pieces together along the edge where they will be joined.

3. Either by hand or using a machine, straight stitch along the side, about ¼ inch (6 mm) in from the raw edge of the fabric (figure 4).

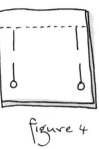

figure 4

4. Lay the pieces out flat, and, using an iron, press the seams to one side (so they lie under a darker fabric, if possible) or open depending on the pattern instructions (figure 5).

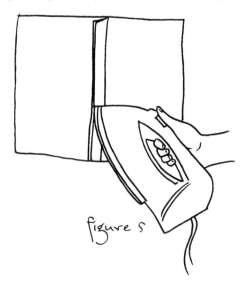

figure 5

Attaching a Border

Many quilts use borders to accentuate or frame the central design. Like piecing, you'll attach a border using the ¼-inch (6 mm) seam allowance and then iron the seams to one side. The steps are fairly similar for adding sashing—strips of fabric that run like a grid between individual quilt units—except that you'll be attaching fabric to both sides of the strip.

1. Following your pattern instructions, cut fabric strips in the correct dimensions for each border of the quilt.

2. Working on a short side of the quilt, pin the border strip to the quilt top with right sides together.

3. Stitch along the edge, using a ¼-inch (6 mm) seam allowance. Press the seam out toward the border (figure 6).

4. Repeat steps 2 and 3 for the quilt's other short side, then for the two long sides (figure 7).

figure 6

figure 7

APPLIQUÉ

Maybe it's that fancy accent mark, but something about "appliqué" sounds a little intimidating. In reality, it couldn't be more basic: the term refers to a process in which a decorative shape is cut from one fabric and stitched on top of another fabric. Once you've cut out your fabric shape (using a pattern from this book or your own design), you'll pin or fuse the shape onto the quilt top and then attach it by machine or hand sewing using decorative stitches. Voila!

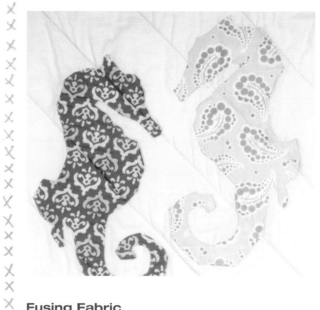

Fusing Fabric

If fusible web isn't already your best friend, it will be soon. There are a number of types on the market, but the paper-backed kind is the best choice for quilting. Basically, fusible web keeps your appliqué shapes from moving while you stitch them in place. And it's super easy to use.

figure 8

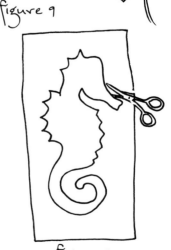

figure 9

figure 10

figure 11

1. Trace the appliqué shape onto the paper backing, keeping in mind that the shape will need to be in reverse of the actual pattern (figure 8).

2. Cut out the tracing and, following the manufacturer's instructions, iron it onto the wrong side of the fabric with the paper side up (figure 9).

3. Using the tracing as a guide, cut out the appliqué shape (figure 10).

4. Peel off the paper backing (figure 11), place the appliqué on the quilt top, and iron it in place. Stitch around the edges of the shape following the pattern instructions.

Turning the Edges

Many of the appliquéd quilts in this book leave the appliqué edges raw for a lovely, if slightly imperfect, finish that frays gently with time and use. Others feature turned-under edges for a clean, professional look. You can spend your days pressing under those tiny seam allowances with a hot iron, and likely scorch the bejeezus out of your fingertips, or you can use freezer paper (see sidebar below). Some folks skip the pressing altogether and use the appliqué stitch (page 19), which turns under the seam allowance and stitches the shape in place at the same time.

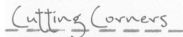

Freezer Pleaser

As it turns out, plastic-coated freezer paper is great for avoiding freezer burn and iron burns. This handy kitchen product can help you turn under appliqué seam-allowance edges before you stitch your shape onto the quilt top. First, trace the appliqué shape onto the dull side of the freezer paper. Cut out the tracing, iron it onto the wrong side of the fabric with the shiny side down (it'll stick to the fabric), and then cut the fabric using the tracing as a guide, adding enough for a seam allowance around the edges. Use spray starch on the seam allowance, clip along the curves, press the edges over onto the freezer paper, and remove the freezer paper. Presto, chango: your appliqué is ready to go.

Sewing the Edges

Once you've secured your appliqué in place—using fusible web or pins—you'll need to finish the edges with a little bit of stitching (see page 19 for the Stitch Glossary). You can hand stitch the stitches indicated in the pattern instructions (we salute you) or just imitate them with your sewing machine; sadly, you won't be able to bluff them all.

If you're planning on leaving the edges raw, use a straight, running, or backstitch to topstitch along the sides of the shape about ¼ inch (6 mm) in from the edge. To avoid fraying, try a thicker stitch, like machine zigzag or satin stitch or hand-worked blanket stitch, around the outside of the shape to cover the raw edge of the fabric.

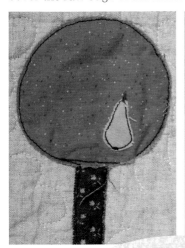

> **66** Try ripping the fabric if you need long strips! Make a short cut about an inch (2.5 cm) in from the edge, and tear off the strip. Then measure the width you need for your strip, make another short cut, and tear the width you need. This works great for cottons. **99**
> —Laurraine Yuyama
> see my quilt on page 71

If you want to turn the appliqué edges under, you'll need to use the freezer paper method or the appliqué stitch, and you'll likely have to work by hand. To make sure your background fabric stays flat, try securing both your appliqué shape and the background fabric in an embroidery hoop.

Cutting Corners

AppliQuilting

Made-up words are the best, aren't they? In some cases, the project instructions will have you add appliqués as part of the final quilting step, as in Monkey Business, page 71. For this process, you'll stack all the quilt layers together (appliqué shape, quilt top, batting, and—depending on the instructions—backing) before you begin to attach the appliqué. The stitching that you do to attach the appliqué to the quilt top will also quilt the layers together in one simple step. You can use embroidery stitches in a similar manner, creating your design on the quilt top and quilting all of the layers together at the same time.

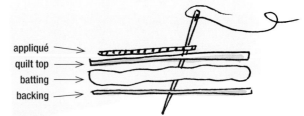

appliqué →
quilt top →
batting →
backing →

EMBROIDERY

Since you can't use beads or buttons to embellish your quilt, given obvious choking hazards, embroidery is a great way to add safe texture and creative interest to your quilt. Compared to appliqué stitching, embroidery stitches are much more decorative in nature. In this process, you're not attaching fabric to fabric; you're simply making decorative stitches through a layer of fabric.

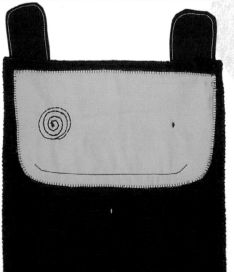

Transferring Embroidery Patterns

Before you get to the stitching, you'll need to do some prep work to transfer the embroidery pattern to your piece of fabric. For light fabrics that you can see through, simply lay the fabric over the design and trace it with a sharp pencil or fabric marker. For darker fabrics, you can transfer the design by using a light box, fabric transfer paper, or drawing the design freehand with a water-soluble fabric marker.

Creating the Stitches

There are whole books dedicated to the subject of embroidery stitches, but our handy Stitch Glossary (page 19) lists all the stitches you'll need for the projects in this book. Thicker than standard sewing thread, embroidery floss or perle cotton are the best choices for this type of needlework, especially if you want all that hard-earned handwork to show up against a background (and trust us, you do!). Refer to the pattern instructions to see how many strands to use; some may ask you to split the embroidery floss down to two or three strands. To make sure your fabric doesn't pucker as you work, you might want to use an embroidery hoop.

66 My first quilting teacher told me this old saying: 'A long thread makes for a lazy girl.' In other words, it's a lot easier to start with a shorter piece of thread than to cut a really, really long piece of thread and wind up with a bunch of knots! I share this advice with all my students and follow it myself as well. 99
—Benares Angeley
see my quilt on page 30

18

Stitch Glossary

Many of the stitches used in appliqué can be used for embroidery, and vice versa. There are a few stitches—like the French knot—that have to be done by hand, but you'll be able to use a sewing machine for many of these.

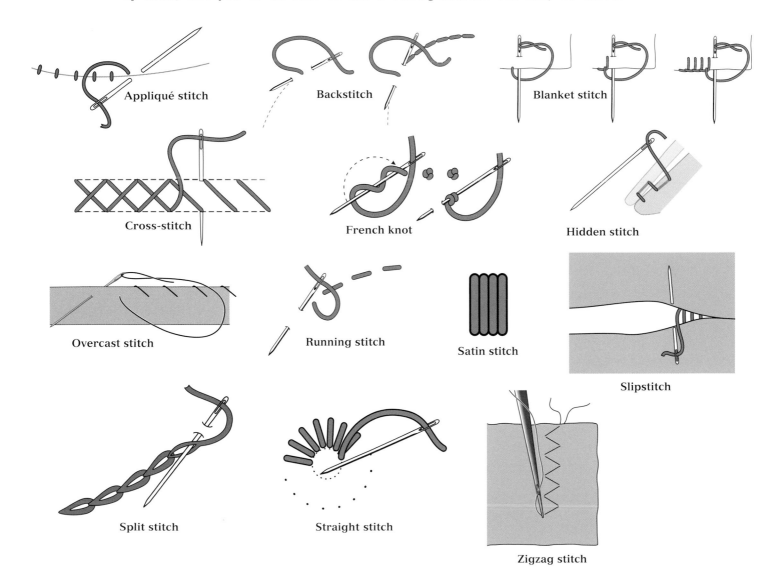

Appliqué stitch

Backstitch

Blanket stitch

Cross-stitch

French knot

Hidden stitch

Overcast stitch

Running stitch

Satin stitch

Slipstitch

Split stitch

Straight stitch

Zigzag stitch

BASTING

Finished your lovingly crafted quilt top? Check. Got your batting and backing? Check. Now, for the moment of truth: putting it all together into one deliciously cozy quilt sandwich. Before you start sewing your layers together, you'll need to stack and baste the quilt top, batting, and backing to make sure they stay flat during the quilting process.

First, iron your layers so they're smooth and free of wrinkles. Lay them out on a flat surface in the following order, with each layer centered on top of the previous one: put your backing, right side down, on the bottom followed by the batting and then your quilt top, with the right side up (figure 12). Starting in the center of the quilt and working out, pin, or baste the layers together with safety or quilting pins spaced about 6 inches (15.2 cm) apart (figure 13). When you've pinned your way around the quilt, take a quick look at the quilt top and the backing to make sure all the layers are smooth and flat.

Note: If you're finishing the edges using the quick-turn method (when you stitch your layers together while inside out and then flip them right side out instead of binding the edges), you'll need to stack your layers in a different order before you baste them. Take a look at page 28 for more information.

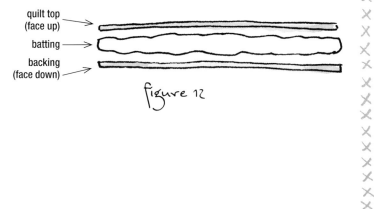

quilt top (face up)

batting

backing (face down)

figure 12

QUILTING

This part of the assembly process is what makes a quilt a quilt. Once your quilt top, batting, and backing have been stacked and basted, your next step is to stitch through the quilt sandwich to connect all the layers and secure the batting in the middle. Sometimes quilt stitching (merely called quilting by those in the know) can be as simple as a grid of straight lines. Other times, the quilt stitching itself is a design element.

As with many other steps in quilt making, quilting can be done by hand or machine, and each method has its own benefits. Whether you're working by machine or by hand, start by planning your stitch pattern. If you're doing something really complicated, you might consider drawing out the pattern on your quilt top with chalk or a water-soluble fabric marker. You have several options when it comes to quilting patterns, and the projects in this book use a wide array of styles.

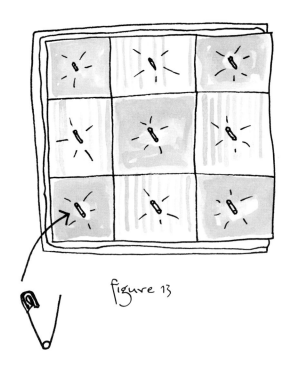

figure 13

Straight-stitch Quilting

Workable by hand and especially by machine (our favorite), straight-stitch quilting is probably the most basic type; it's the same type of stitch you used in piecing the quilt and other standard sewing tasks. If you're straight stitching by hand (also called a running stitch), keep your stitches short and even. For a clean finish, pull your knots through so they are hidden in the batting. On your machine, you might need to loosen the needle tension and lengthen the stitch to accommodate the thick layers. Since it can sometimes be difficult to handle all those thick layers, especially if your quilt sandwich has lots of, er…condiments, rolling up the edges can help you access the whole quilt in sections (figure 14).

figure 14

Using a straight stitch, you have some further options. Stitch in the ditch is a process that involves stitching along the seam lines of the quilt top's pieced sections, hiding your quilting stitches in the piecing seams.

You can also use the straight stitch to outline various design elements—such as appliqué or pieced shapes—to accentuate those lovingly crafted details.

For a classic geometric finish, straight stitch parallel lines across the quilt top using a handy quilt bar attachment or

make a statement by creating decorative shapes, like circles or swirls, to oppose the straight lines of the quilt top.

Feeling extra creative and ambitious? Try creating shapes to go along with the theme of your quilt, like the bananas and numbers in Monkey Business (page 71).

Free-Motion Quilting

A perfect approach for independent types, free-motion quilting means you have complete control of the quilting stitch pattern, giving your project oodles of texture and even more handmade appeal (if that's possible). For free-motion quilting on the machine, a darning foot—which has a circular opening for the needle to pass through—can help. You'll also need to disengage the automatic feed mechanism (called feed dogs in some machine manuals); in this method, you control the movement of the fabric, and thus the shape of the stitch, by using two hands to spread the fabric out flat under the needle (figure 15). Guide the fabric to create any shape you like: free-form clouds, teensy circles, or winding doodles.

figure 15

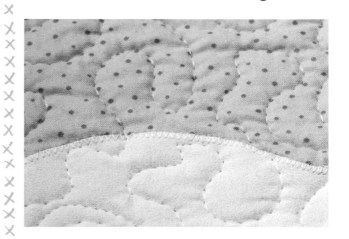

Tying

Here's a technique that speaks to the shortcut lover in us all, and it's okay to love shortcuts. Instead of stitching across the quilt, tying involves connecting the quilt layers with a few stitches placed in a grid and tied, with the knots on the top of the quilt. You can use embroidery floss, perle cotton, or yarn for this process, depending on the look you're going for. The end result has a charming, folksy feel that is undeniably handmade.

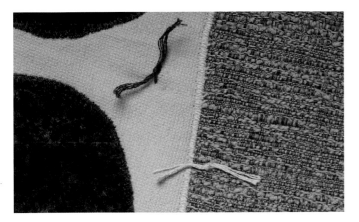

1. Use a ruler and chalk to mark a grid on your basted quilt top—you'll place your stitches where the lines intersect—or place the ties randomly, as long as they're a suitable distance apart. Check your batting for spacing suggestions, but 2 to 6 inches (5 to 15.2 cm) apart should be enough.

2. Thread a sharp hand-sewing needle with yarn (or whatever material you're using).

3. Stitch straight down through the quilt layers and then back up, making sure the layers don't shift as you work.

4. Tie the yarn tails in a knot—a square knot works well (figure 16)—and then trim them to ¾ to 1 inch (1.9 to 2.5 cm) long. Repeat steps 3 and 4 for each tie.

figure 16

Cutting Corners

Tying the Knots

If you're creating a lot of ties on your quilt top, use a single long piece of floss to create the stitches in a row instead of stitching each tie individually. Create a stitch at each intersection across the row, leaving extra floss between each stitch. Then cut the floss at the midpoint between each stitch and use the tails to tie knots at each point.

Finishing Up

By this point in the process, you've probably got something that actually looks like a quilt (bravo!). But no premature flaunting: you've got a few more steps before your project is ready for its big debut.

BINDING

There's no clear way to fit this step into our nifty sandwich metaphor—darn it—but the results might lead to an exotic culinary invention. In quilting, it's a little less exciting; binding refers to the process of covering the edges of the quilt with a strip of either single- or double-layered fabric so you no longer see the individual quilt layers. When you've finished the binding, your work is done…although you'll need to follow up with a requisite amount of gloating. That process is easy: show your creation off to anyone who'll look!

Making Your Own Binding

You can buy premade binding at the fabric store—although your color and width options might be limited—or you can make your own, in which case you'll have plenty of fabrics and widths to choose from. Some designers make a separate length of binding for each edge, although the majority make one very long length of binding and attach it around all of the edges in one fell swoop. The instructions will tell you to cut your binding strips either lengthwise, crossgrain, or on the bias—diagonally across the length of the fabric (figure 17). Bias-cut binding strips have a little more stretch to them, but they do require more fabric.

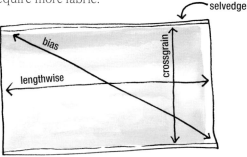

figure 17

1. To figure out how long your strip will need to be, add the lengths of the top, bottom, left, and right edges of the quilt, plus a few inches extra.

2. Once you've calculated the length you need, cut your strips following the recommended width in the pattern instructions.

3. To connect the strips together, you have two options. For the first method, pin and stitch the short ends together, with right sides facing, until you have one long strip, then press the seams open (figure 18).

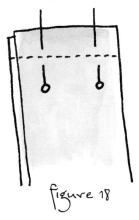

figure 18

For the second method, pin the short ends together at a right angle, with right sides facing, and stitch diagonally across the corner (figure 19). Trim the seam allowance and press the seams open.

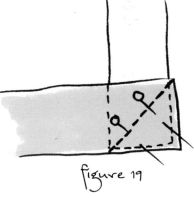

figure 19

Single Binding with Mitered Corners

The project instructions will tell you whether to use single-fold or double-fold binding, but feel free to pick the method that works best for you. If you're like the majority of quilters, you'll probably make one strip of binding that's long enough

to wrap around the entire quilt. When you reach a corner on the quilt, you need a special way to wrap the binding so that it looks neat and lies flat. In these steps, we'll cover mitered corners—which create a clean diagonal pleat in the binding at each corner—but butted corners (page 26) might be even easier if you're new to working with binding.

1. Once you've quilted the layers together, lay the quilt completely flat and trim the edges so the quilt top, batting, and backing are all the same size.

2. Starting midway on one edge or near a corner, pin and then stitch the right side of the batting to the right side of the fabric, folding over the starting edge (figure 20). Use the seam allowance width that's indicated in the instructions.

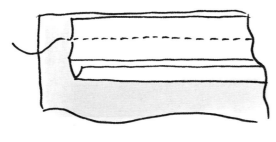

figure 20

3. Stop stitching as you approach the corner, and clip the threads to remove the quilt from the machine. Fold the binding straight up over itself so a 45° angle forms at the corner (figure 21).

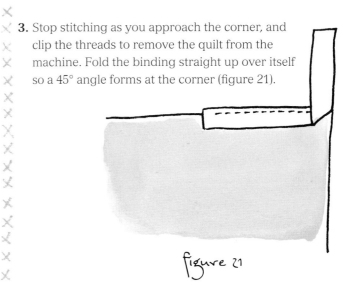

figure 21

4. Fold the binding straight down so it's even with the edge of the quilt, and then continue pinning and stitching the binding in place (figure 22). Continue working your way around the quilt, using the same process for the rest of the corners.

figure 22

5. As you near your starting point, stitch your binding strip over the folded-over starting edge of the binding strip. There's no need to fold back the raw edge at the very end of the binding strip—it'll soon be hidden.

6. Fold the binding strip over the edges—but not too tightly—to the back of the quilt. Turn under the raw edge just enough to cover the seam that you just stitched. (This edge will already be folded to the wrong side if you're using purchased binding, and you already have a folded edge if you're using double-fold binding.) Place the prepared edge just barely over the seam line that attached the binding, and pin it down along each edge. Create diagonal folds at each corner and then pin the corners in place.

7. Use a slipstitch by hand (page 19) or stitch in the ditch—working from the top of the quilt—using your machine to attach the binding to the back of the quilt (figure 23).

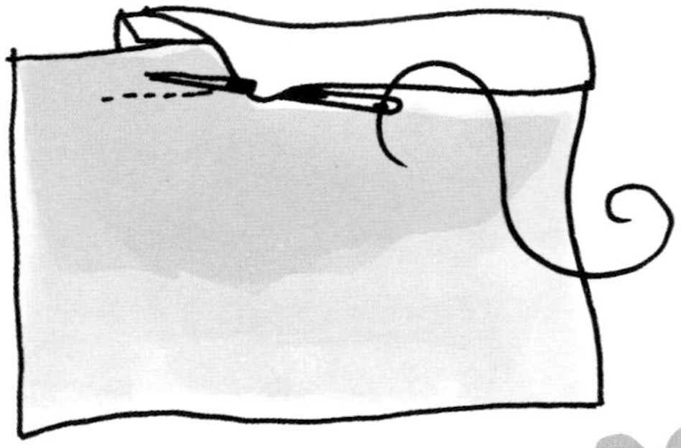

figure 23

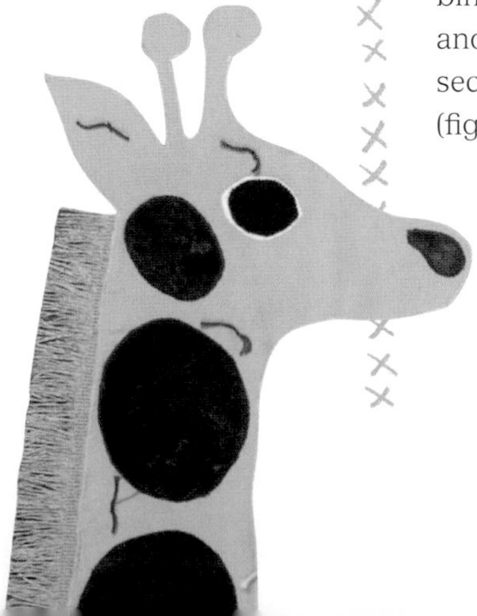

Butted Corners

Maybe butted corners aren't quite as clean and neat as mitered corners, but those quilt corners are probably going to end up covered in baby drool anyway, right?

1. Working one edge at a time (instead of a continuous strip), pin and then stitch binding along the two short edges on the right side of the quilt.

2. Fold the binding to the back, tuck under the raw edge if the binding is single-fold, and then stitch it down on the back using the slipstitch or stitching in the ditch of the seam you just created (figure 24).

3. Measure and then cut the length you'll need for the long edges of the quilt, adding a little extra to each end, and attach binding to the edges as you did with the short edges.

4. Turn under the extra binding at each end and use a slipstitch to secure the ends closed (figure 25).

figure 24

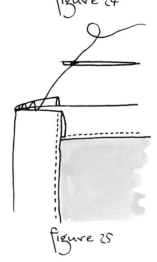

figure 25

Double-layer Binding

While this method may only initially appeal to certain overachievers among us (ahem, we're not mentioning names), the steps are essentially the same as using a single-layer binding. This process can also extend the life of your quilt; the edges will stand up much better to wear, tear, and teething. Projects that use double-layer binding will tell you how wide to cut your strips, but in general, your strips will need to be about six times wider than the final binding width you're planning.

1. Following the pattern instructions, cut the strips and then sew them together.

2. Fold the binding strip in half lengthwise with wrong sides together and then pin it to the right side of the quilt top, lining up the raw edges (figure 26).

figure 26

3. Stitch the binding in place using the recommended seam allowance, mitering the corners (although you can also use this technique with butted corners) as you work around the quilt.

4. Fold the binding to the back of the quilt, and then pin and stitch it in place. Since the fabric has been folded in half, you don't have to worry about turning under any raw edges (figure 27).

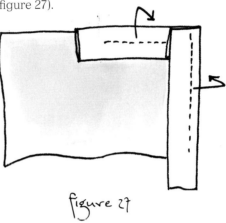

figure 27

Cutting Corners

In a Bind

If you're feeling plucky, you could try binding both sides of the quilt at the same time. To do this, press under the seam allowance on both sides of your binding strip. Fold the strip over the edges of the quilt, and then pin and topstitch along the edge, making sure you stitch through all the layers, stopping a few inches (cm) short of where you started attaching the binding. Fold under the loose end of the binding strip, and pin it over your starting point. Continue stitching to the end of your binding strip and then a little beyond that, just to be safe.

binding

quilt layers

Quick Turning a Quilt

Okay, the secret's out on this super handy quilting shortcut. This process allows you to skip binding altogether, and you're left with edges that are clean, if not quite as crisp as bound edges. This technique works particularly well if you plan on tying your quilt.

1. Stack your quilt by placing the batting on the bottom followed by the backing, with right side up, and the quilt top, centered with the right side down (figure 28).

2. Pin the layers together along the edges, placing a few pins in the middle of the quilt to keep the layers smooth.

3. Stitch almost all the way around the outside edge of the quilt, using a ½-inch (1.3 cm) seam allowance. Leave about 10 inches (25.4 cm) unstitched; you'll use this opening to turn the quilt through (figure 29). If your quilt is especially large or thick, you may need a bigger opening.

4. Trim along the edges so all three layers are the same size, and cut across the corners to decrease bulk. Turn the quilt right side out and hand stitch the opening closed (figure 30).

5. Baste the quilt using pins, and then quilt, or tie, the layers.

quilt top (face down)

backing (face up)

batting

10 inches (25.4 cm)

figure 28

figure 29

figure 30

HANGING

Some of the projects in this book are meant to be enjoyed sans drool. Creating a baby quilt wall hanging—an art quilt of sorts—opens up a whole other world of design possibilities.

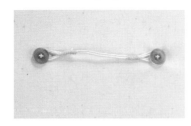

If your quilt has heavy interfacing or backing, as with the Trilogy on page 107, add buttons and a simple strand of elastic to create a hanger.

If your quilt is a little bigger, consider adding a sleeve for a dowel rod. Cut a strip of fabric that's about 4 inches (10.2 cm) wide and almost as long as your quilt's width. Turn and stitch under the short raw edges, and then pin and stitch the long edges together with right sides facing (figure 31). Turn the sleeve right side out and place it seam side down on the backing. Pin and hand stitch the sleeve in place along the top and bottom edges (figure 32). The sleeve will accommodate most dowel rods, or slide ribbon through the sleeve for an easy transition to a superhero cape.

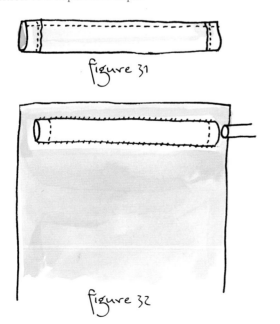

figure 31

figure 32

CLEANING (A.K.A. GACK ATTACK)

Messy baby + handmade quilt = laundry duty. Inevitably, spills and accidents follow babies no matter where they roam. So what's the best way to clean a messy quilt? Wash your quilt in cold water to keep the colors from fading, and tumble dry on low or let it hang to dry. For set-in stains, use bleach-free stain remover directly on the quilt, let it sit for a few hours, and then wash it by hand or in a cold-water wash cycle. For a more gentle cleaning method, sprinkle baking soda on the stained area and then pour on some club soda. Let the club soda and baking soda foam for a few seconds, then gently scrub the area with an old toothbrush.

If baby has extra sensitive skin, avoid using detergent with phosphates, which will be listed in the soap ingredients. If your quilt needs a little freshening up, just hang it outside for a few hours (out of direct sunlight to avoid fading), and let nature do its thing.

Name Games

A baby quilt is a unique, one-of-a-kind creation, just like its intended recipient. Use embroidery stitching, a permanent fabric marker, or a preprinted fabric tag to personalize your baby quilt. Record baby's name, weight, and date of arrival, a heartfelt message, or information about you, the artist, to make those special memories last even longer.

Red Shoe Dog

One of the undeniable charms of this quilt is its quirky, folksy look; the effect is created with ties and raw-edged appliqué shapes, both of which mean less work for you. To simplify the process even further, both the background and the foreground are comprised of just a few large, simple appliqués.

Benares
Angeley

Fabric

All fabric is cotton, 44 inches (111.8 cm) wide.

QUILT TOP
1 yard (0.9 m) of blue small print or slightly textured surface
1 yard (0.9 m) of golden yellow
¼ yard (0.2 m) of red-and-white print
1 yard (0.9 m) of black

APPLIQUÉS
¼ yard (0.2 m) each of black and blue for the bird
¼ yard (0.2 m) of red for the bird and shoes
1 yard (0.9 m) of brown print for all three dogs
1 yard (0.9 m) of golden yellow for the stars and crown

QUILT BACKING
2 yards (1.8 m) of blue

BINDING
Pieced scraps or a yard (0.9 m) cut in strips along the length

Notions & Such

Quilting Tool Kit (see page 11)

Appliqué patterns (see page 139)

100% cotton-covered polyester sewing thread: black, blue, gray, and yellow

Low-loft cotton batting

Embroidery needle

Tapestry needle

Large embroidery hoop

Pattern transfer materials and tools

Skein each of perle cotton or embroidery floss*: black, brown, and red

Skein of gray wool yarn for tying the quilt

Use two strands if you embroider with floss.

Finished Size

43 x 57 inches (109.2 x 144.8 cm)

Instructions

This quilt doesn't have any seam allowances except for the quilt top background and the binding.

Get Scrappy

1 Cut the fabric for the quilt top background using the patterns.

2 Sew a longer side of the blue print rectangle to a matching side of the golden yellow rectangle, using a straight stitch on your sewing machine. Press these—and all other seam allowances—open when constructing your quilt.

3 Using the whole quilt template (see figure 1) as a guide, baste the red-and-white print rolling hill shape over the seam line for the blue and golden yellow, with all of the fabrics right side up. Don't turn under the raw fabric edges. Secure the edges of the red piece to the background with the red perle cotton or embroidery floss and embroidered overcast stitches. Remove the basting.

figure 1

4 Baste the black (rolling cloud) shape over the upper edge of the golden yellow fabric. Secure the raw, wavy edge of the black shape to the golden yellow shape with the black perle cotton or embroidery floss, and embroider overcast stitches. Remove the basting.

Snippet
The finished quilt features shoes and a bird that are cut from a red curtain. The blue cloth used for part of the quilt top background is vintage upholstery fabric, and the golden yellow stars and background are from a piece of hand-dyed silk.

Way to Appliqué!

5 Trace the appliqué patterns on page 139–140 to make templates for the birds, crown, dogs, shoes, and stars. Don't add seam allowances. Cut these out of the appropriate fabric, flipping over the templates before cutting out some of the shapes so that you have some facing the opposite direction.

6 Baste all of the appliqués to the quilt top background. Choose embroidery floss, perle cotton, or sewing thread in matching colors to appliqué each piece to your quilt. Use embroidered overcast stitches to sew the edges to the background. Hold the basted appliqué and background fabric taut in an embroidery hoop while you stitch. Remove the basting.

Sew It Up

7 Cut the batting and the blue backing fabric (or piece scraps). Stack and baste the quilt layers together.

8 Tie the quilt layers together with the yarn. Benares used 100 percent wool yarn so that the ties would full (shrink or felt) when she washed the finished quilt. This fulling makes for very strong ties on the quilt top.

It's a Wrap

9 Bind the quilt with your desired method with gray sewing thread. Benares cut 5-Inch-wide (12.7 cm) strips and used the double-fold binding technique with a ¾-inch (1.9 cm) seam allowance.

Snippet
Think carefully about how your finished quilt will need to be laundered as your fabric choices and stitching may greatly affect the results.

Benares Angeley

EARLIEST MEMORY: When I was three years old, my brother was born. I drew him a picture of a watermelon to welcome him to our family.

TACKIEST THING I EVER MADE: A hot pink miniskirt and matching halter top, with a pattern on the fabric that looked like splattered black paint. I made it when I was ten years old and wore it for the next three or four years until it fell apart at the seams.

SEWING/QUILTING IDOL: Harriet Powers and my great-grandmother.

Inspire Me!

Got a future Tour-de-France-er on your hands? Instead of a bone, give your dog a bicycle.

Life Savers

A bed sheet or printed fabric that features a colorful repeating pattern, such as the circles on the purchased duvet cover used in this project, is an ideal starting point for a quilt top. Just cut around the motif to make a square, and use that as the center of each block. You can even substitute or add circles or motifs from other fabrics.

Malka Dubrawsky

Fabric

All fabric is cotton, 44 inches (111.8 cm) wide.

QUILT TOP
   Bedsheet, duvet cover, or yardage printed with a repeating motif in a variety of sizes

   ¼ yard (0.2 m) each of 27 different fabrics, 70 to 80% solids and 20 to 30% prints, for the pieced strips: 8 blues, 8 greens, 4 oranges, 2 pinks, 3 reds, and 2 yellows

BACKING
   1 ½ yards (1.4 m) of a coordinating yellow-and-white print

BINDING
   ¼ yard (0.2 m) of a coordinating blue print

Notions & Such

Quilting Tool Kit (see page 11)

Tracing paper or clear template material

Low-loft cotton batting

All-purpose cotton-wrapped white sewing thread

White machine-quilting thread

Finished Size

36 x 45 inches (91.4 x 114.3 cm)

Instructions

All of the seam allowances are ¼ inch (6 mm) wide.

Get Scrappy

1 Cut the bed sheet, duvet cover, or yardage into 20 squares that are all centered around a circle (or other motif). Include a border beyond the motif of at least ¼ inch (6 mm) for a seam allowance (see figure 1). Pick motifs of different dimensions so that you have center squares in several sizes. Malka used circles with diameters of 2, 3½, 4, and 6¼ inches (5, 8.9, 10.2, and 15.9 cm).

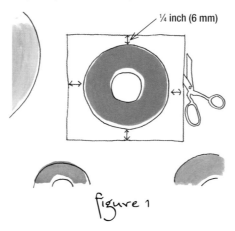

¼ inch (6 mm)

figure 1

2 Cut 12-inch-long (30.5 cm) strips freehand from the 27 lengths of fabric you chose for piecing. Let the width of these strips range from 1 to 5 inches (2.5 to 12.7 cm) wide.

Building Blocks

3 Sew a lengthwise edge of a fabric strip to an edge of a center square with right sides together. Use the white sewing thread for all of the piecing and for joining the blocks together in later steps. Press the seam allowances to one side, and trim off the excess length of the strip beyond the seam line. Sew a second strip perpendicular to the first strip, and also trim it off at the end of the seam.

4 Add two more strips, one at a time, to complete the square.

5 Continue adding strips until you have a block that measures 9½ inches (24.1 cm) square. You don't need to measure the block, but if you'd like reassurance, cut a 9½-inch (24.1 cm) square from the tracing paper or template material, and lay it on top of the block to check the size. If the block is too large, use the tracing paper as a pattern piece: shift the block around underneath this pattern piece until you like the composition of your block, and then trim off the excess fabric so that the block is the same size as the paper. Make 19 more blocks.

figure 2

Sew It Up

6 Refer to the whole quilt illustration (see figure 2) throughout the rest of these instructions. Join four blocks to make an 18½-inch (47 cm) square. As you assemble the blocks, press the seam allowances together and toward one side. If your four-patch is too small, add a strip of fabric along the edge that comes up short. If it's too big, use a ruler and rotary cutter to trim it to size.

7 Assemble more blocks. When you have an eight-patch, it needs to measure 18½ x 36½-inches (47 x 92.7 cm). Your 16-block piece should be 36½ inches (92.7 cm) square. Make a row with the last blocks, and join it to the 16-patch to finish the top.

8 Stack and baste the quilt layers together.

9 Switch to the white quilting thread, and quilt a spiral pattern inside a colored circle in the center of a 9½-inch (24.1 cm) block. Quilt the outside edge of the same circle, and then stitch the surrounding strips in concentric lines spaced ¼ inch (6 mm) apart. Quilt each circle block independently, always starting in the center of the circle.

It's a Wrap

10 Bind the quilt with your desired method. Malka started with 1½-inch-wide (3.8 cm) strips to make a single-fold binding using ¼-inch (6 mm) seam allowances and mitered corners.

Snippet

Embrace the opportunity to cut fabric like you would draw a freehand line. You'll be amazed by how well you can cut a straight line without a ruler, using only a rotary cutter and self-healing mat.

BEHIND THE SEAMS WITH
✕✕✕✕✕✕✕✕✕✕✕✕✕✕✕✕✕✕✕✕✕✕✕✕✕✕
Malka Dubrawsky

FIRST SEWING PROJECT: I made a jumper for myself in college. That's when I taught myself to sew.

SEWING/QUILTING IDOL: I have a host of idols depending on the fiber arena, but in terms of quilting, I'd have to list Nancy Crow.

HOW MUCH FABRIC HAVE YOU ACCUMULATED? I should plead the Fifth Amendment, but I'll admit that I do have an entire walk-in closet devoted to materials.

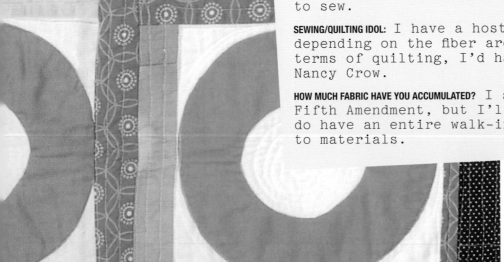

Woodland Creatures

Aimee Ray

Surround your favorite bambino with friendly woodland creatures embroidered on a quilted bumper. Stuffed with foam instead of standard quilt batting, this project features a neat way to add dimension to your appliqué shapes.

figure 1

Cutting Chart

Fabric	Quantity to cut	Size
White	(2)	30" x 6" (76.2 x 15.2 cm)
	(2)	54" x 6" (137.2 x 15.2 cm)
Aqua	(2)	30" x 4" (76.2 x 10.2 cm)
	(2)	54" x 4" (137.2 x 10.2 cm)
Light green	(2)	30" x $3^1/2$" (76.2 x 8.9 cm)
	(2)	54" x $3^1/2$" (137.2 x 8.9 cm)
Dark green print	(2)	30" x 12" (76.2 x 30.5 cm)
	(2)	54" x 12" (137.2 x 30.5 cm)

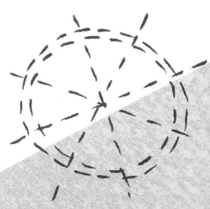

Fabric

All fabric is cotton, 44 inches (111.8 cm) wide.

TOP
1½ yards (1.4 m) each of aqua, light green, and white

APPLIQUÉS
Five 10-inch (25.4 cm) squares of three to five different patterned fabrics in various shades of green for the treetops

BACKING
1½ yards (1.4 m) of dark green print

Notions & Such

Quilting Tool Kit (see page 11)

Embroidery patterns (page 138)

2 packages of ½-inch-wide (1.3 cm) light green double-fold bias tape

24 x 82 x 1 inch (61 x 208.3 x 2.5 cm) foam sheet

Embroidery needle and hoop

All-purpose cotton-wrapped sewing thread: aqua, light green, and white

Skein each of embroidery floss: dark brown and light brown

Finished Size

Sides: two 52 x 10-inch (132.1 x 25.4 cm) pads

Ends: two 28 x 10-inch (71.1 x 25.4 cm) pads

Fits a 52 x 28-inch (132.1 x 71.1 cm) crib

Instructions

All of the seam allowances are ½ inch (1.3 cm) wide.

Get Scrappy

1. Cut two 52 x 10-inch (132.1 x 25.4 cm) pieces and two 28 x 10-inch (71.1 x 25.4 cm) pieces from the foam sheet, and all of the fabric for the tops and backings (see the cutting chart).

2. Refer to the whole quilt template (see figure 1) throughout these instructions. Machine stitch an aqua strip to the top and a light green strip to the bottom of each white strip, using the matching color sewing thread and straight stitches.

Way to Appliqué!

3. Enlarge the oval tree shapes on the whole quilt template, and cut one of each from the green fabric squares. Pin the appliqué treetop shapes to the assembled bumper tops, then attach them using an appliqué stitch. For appliqués with added dimension, take a look at the snippet on the following page.

Embroider This!

4. Enlarge and transfer the embroidery patterns to the fabric. Embroider the tree trunks and animal designs using a split stitch.

Sew It Up

5 Cut two 24-inch-long (61 cm) pieces of bias tape for each bumper, to make ties. Join the matching quilt tops and backings with their right sides together. Fold the ties in half lengthwise, and tuck one inside two adjacent corners of each bumper so that the fold is in the seam allowance (see figure 2).

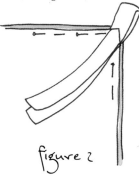

figure 2

6 Sew around the two long edges and one short edge of each bumper cover, using a sewing machine straight stitch. Trim the corners diagonally to remove the extra fabric. Begin turning a cover, inserting one end of the cut-to-fit foam inside, and then continuing to turn the cover right side out, right over the foam. Turn the rest of the covers in the same way.

7 Sew the open ends of each bumper closed with hidden stitches.

Snippet

Here is an easy way to make smooth, rounded, and dimensional appliqués for your treetops. Cut two pieces of matching fabric for each green oval. Sew them together with right sides facing, leaving a 1-inch (2.5 cm) opening unsewn. Clip through the seam allowances intermittently around the seam line. Turn each oval right side out, and tuck the seam allowance into the hole. Stuff the oval with a bit of batting and then sew the opening closed along the seam line.

BEHIND THE SEAMS WITH
x x x x x x x x x x x x x x
Aimee Ray

SEE MORE OF MY STUFF AT: www.dreamfollow.com

MY NEXT QUILTING PROJECT: I want to make mini embroidered quilts and pillows for my Blythe dolls.

WHAT IS YOUR FAVORITE PART OF QUILTING? Designing. I can come up with a million ideas, but actually getting them done is another story.

DESCRIBE YOUR ADDICTION TO FABRIC: If you don't have every color you can think of, it's not enough.

Blowing Bubbles

Marné Cales

Simple appliquéd circles make quick and easy design elements that are just right for showcasing special fabric scraps. Substituting puffy yo-yos for the appliqué circles will give the quilt an entirely different texture and look.

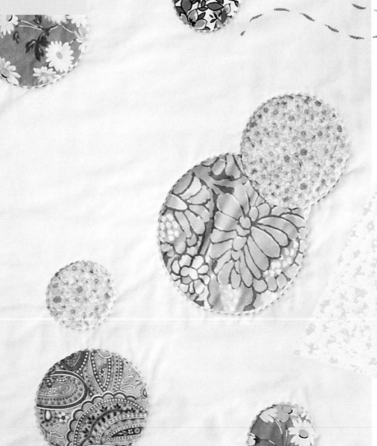

Fabric

All fabric is cotton, 44 inches (111.8 cm) wide.

QUILT TOP
1⅛ yards (1 m) of light blue for the background
¼ yard (0.3 m) each of six assorted prints for the appliqué circles: blue, green, and yellow*

BACKING
1⅜ yards (1.3 m) of a blue floral print

BINDING
⅜ yard (0.4 m) of green-and-white-dot print

Marné used a blue medium-print paisley, blue medium-print floral, green small-print floral, green medium-print floral, yellow medium-print floral, and yellow small-print floral.

Notions & Such

Quilting Tool Kit (see page 11)

Medium-loft cotton batting

All-purpose, cotton-wrapped medium-gray sewing thread

Bright turquoise cotton quilting thread

Sheet of 12-inch-square (30.5 cm) cardstock for method A

3 sheets of 12-inch-square (30.5 cm) cardstock for method B

Large embroidery hoop or hand-quilting frame

Finished Size

36 x 44 inches (91.5 x 111.8 cm)

Instructions

The appliqué seam allowances are ½ inch (1.3 cm) wide. All other seam allowances are ¼ inch (6 mm) wide.

Get Scrappy

1 Cut a 37 x 44-inch (94 x 111.8 cm) rectangle from the light blue fabric for the quilt top background. Cut another rectangle of the same size from the blue floral fabric for the backing.

2 Cut out three circles from the cardstock: a 2-inch (5 cm), 3-inch (7.6 cm), and a 4-inch (10.2 cm) circle.

3 Cut circles from the appliqué fabric, using the cardstock circles as templates and adding a ½-inch (1.3 cm) seam allowance as you cut out each fabric circle.

Appliqué Cutting Chart

Fabric color	4-inch-diameter (10.2 cm) circle	3-inch-diameter (7.6 cm) circle	2-inch-diameter (5 cm) circle
Green small-print floral	(1)	(1)	(3)
Green medium-print floral	(1)	(2)	(2)
Blue medium-print floral	(1)	(1)	(3)
Yellow medium-print floral	(1)	(1)	(3)
Yellow small-print floral	(1)	(1)	(3)
Blue medium-print paisley	(0)	(1)	(2)

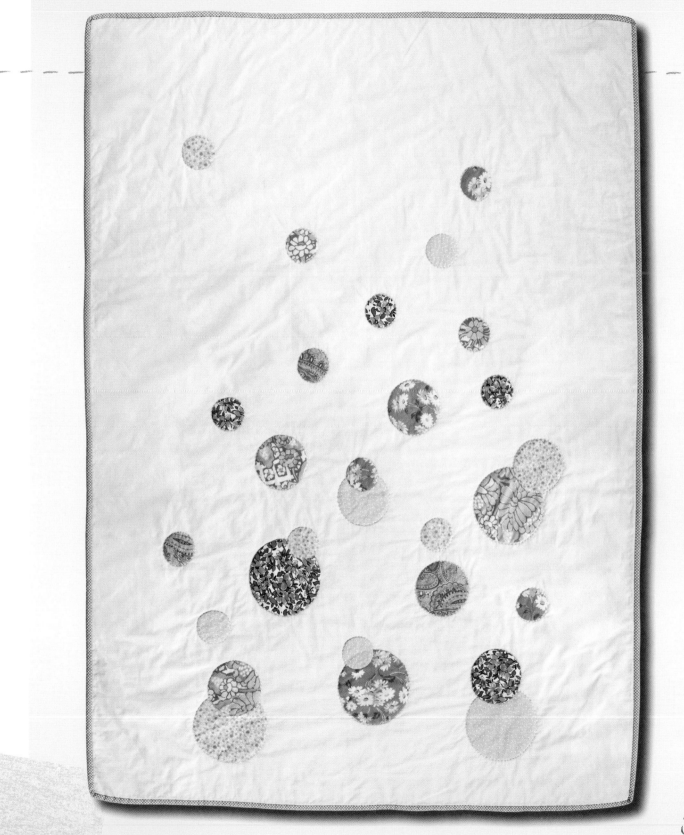

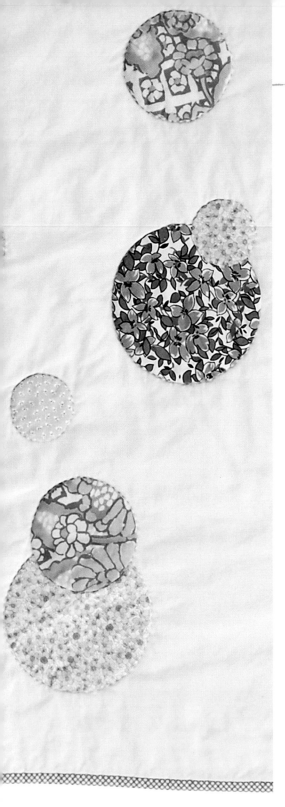

Way to Appliqué!

4 Place the 4-inch (10.2 cm) cardstock circle on the wrong side of one of the large fabric circles. Thread a needle with a length of the sewing thread that's knotted at one end. Sew long running stitches around the perimeter of the fabric circle, in the middle of the seam allowance width.

5 Pull the thread tight, so that the fabric is taut around the cardstock. Tie off the thread. Press the circle well—on both sides—with a hot iron. Carefully remove the cardstock template so that you can use it to prepare the rest of the 4-inch (10.2 cm) circle appliqués. Prepare the rest of the appliqués—in all sizes.

6 Using the project photograph as a guide for placement, arrange the circles on the quilt top, with the larger circles toward the bottom and the smaller circles at the top, overlapping a few here and there. Pin the circles in place.

7 Sew around the edge of a circle that's by itself, using appliqué stitches.

8 Attach the rest of the circles, paying attention to the order when stitching overlapped appliqués: Carefully remove the pins around the top circle where it overlaps the bottom circle, and sew all the way around the bottom circle first.

Sew It Up

9 Stack and baste the quilt layers together.

10 Quilt around all the circles with the quilting thread.

Snippet

To appliqué your circles, you may want to use appliqué pins (sometimes called sequin pins) around the edges of each circle. Appliqué pins are very short so the tips are less likely to catch your sewing thread as you stitch. To avoid pricking yourself as you work, insert them so that the sharp ends point to the center of each circle.

It's a Wrap

11 Cut strips along the width of the binding fabric, and bind the quilt with your desired method. Marné started with 2-inch-wide (5 cm) strips to make a double-fold binding. She attached it with a ¼-inch (6 mm) seam allowance and used mitered corners.

Inspire Me!

Add some texture to your quilt with yo-yos instead of appliqué circles. To make a yo-yo, just cut out a circle of fabric twice the diameter that you want your finished yo-yo to be, turn the edges under ¼ inch (6 mm), run gathering stitches all the way around, and pull the thread to gather the edges underneath.

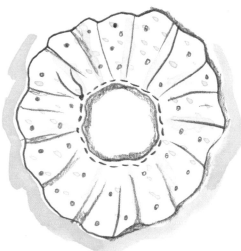

BEHIND THE SEAMS WITH

xxxxxxxxx xxxxxxxxxx

Marné Cales

PLACE I GO FOR INSPIRATION: Outside! All of nature inspires me: flowers, trees, a really bright blue sky, birds (including my pet chickens), animals, everything!

ONE WORD THAT BEST DESCRIBES YOUR ARTISTIC STYLE: Fresh or clean, I can't choose just one!

WHAT IS YOUR FAVORITE PART OF QUILTING: I love designing, but nothing is as satisfying as doing the final hand stitching when finishing the binding.

Intersection

Asymmetrical lines and offset fabric strips combine to create a simple, yet striking design. Perfect angles aren't important in this quilt. Let the simple pieced strips set the pattern and then follow the seams outward.

Laura Ducommun

Fabric

All fabric is cotton, 44 inches (111.8 cm) wide.

QUILT TOP
2 yards (1.8 m) of pink fabric
10 to 15 fat quarters or fabric pieces at least 3 inches (7.6 cm) wide: pink, purple, and red, plus a few blues, browns, and multicolored prints

BACKING
2 yards (1.8 m) of a large print

BINDING
⅜ yard (0.4 m) red-and-white print

Notions & Such

Quilting Tool Kit (see page 11)
Low-loft batting
Water-soluble fabric pen or fabric chalk pencil
All-purpose cotton-wrapped white sewing thread
White cotton quilting thread

Finished Size

42 x 50 inches (106.7 x 127 cm)

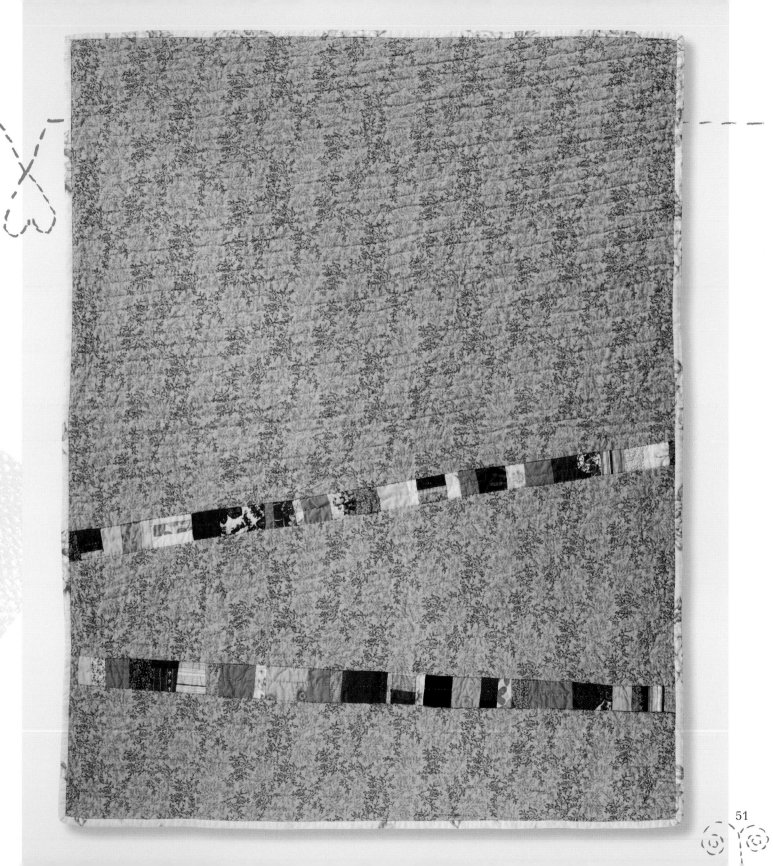

figure 1

figure 2

Instructions

All of the seam allowances are ¼ inch (6 mm) wide.

Get Scrappy

1   Refer to the whole quilt template (see figure 1) throughout these instructions. Cut the fat quarters or fabric scraps to different lengths and at least 3 inches (7.6 cm) wide. You can work with smaller pieces: simply sew them together to create the size you want.

2   Sew the pieces together by chaining them through your sewing machine. Keep the fabric order random. Continue joining the pieces until you have two long strips. Trim the edges so that both are 2½ x 45 inches (6.4 x 114.3 cm).

3   Cut the top fabric so it's 42 x 50 inches (106.7 x 127 cm). Now cut it into three pieces with diagonal lines. Don't worry if the angles aren't exactly as shown in figure 1.

Sew It Up

4   Sew the multi-fabric strips between the three large pieces. The strips will make the top larger, so again trim it to 42 x 50 inches (106.7 x 127 cm).

5   Stack and baste the quilt layers together.

6   Draw the first quilt line on the pink fabric above the top pieced strip. Use the water-soluble fabric pen, and follow the angle of the seam line. Continue drawing parallel lines ¾ inch (1.9 cm) apart all the way to the top of the quilt. Do the same on the bottom of the quilt. In the middle area (between the two multi-fabric strips), draw the lines parallel to both seam lines, and work your way in so that the lines meet somewhere in the middle to create angled points (see figure 2).

7 Quilt the layers together using the white quilting thread. Don't worry about each line being perfectly straight or exactly ¾ inch (1.9 cm) apart. Follow your drawn lines, and have fun.

It's a Wrap

8 Bind your quilt with your desired method. Laura cut a 2-inch-wide (5 cm) strip and used the double-fold binding technique with mitered corners.

BEHIND THE SEAMS WITH

Laura Ducommun

SEE MORE OF MY WORK AT: www.lkdDesigns.etsy.com.

EARLIEST MEMORY: Living in the Philippines. My dad was stationed in Subic Bay, and I remember laying in the kiddie pool in the backyard on Christmas day.

FIRST SEWING PROJECT: Making clothes for my Barbie dolls with my mom.

ONE WORD THAT BEST DESCRIBES YOUR ARTISTIC STYLE: Modern.

Good Night, Moon
Good Morning, Sun

Jude
Stuecker

Variety is the spice of life, and a two-sided quilt is twice as nice to give and receive. Because this is a double-sided quilt, the measuring, cutting, and seams need to be very precise. Fortunately this should be fairly easy since the only piecing you need to do is attaching the border.

Fabric

All fabric is cotton, 44 inches wide (111.8 cm).

QUILT TOP AND BACKING

1½ yards (1.4 m) each of light and dark blue background fabric: light blue for Good Morning and dark blue for Good Night

APPLIQUÉS

½ yard (0.5 m) of each: brown for both tree limbs, dark brown for the owl's head and wings, and red for the songbird's body

¼ yard (0.2 m) of each: green for all of the leaves, orange print for the songbird's wings, medium brown for the owl's body, and light brown for the owl's face

¼ yard (0.2 m) of each for the words: brown for Good Morning, red for Good Night

Small scraps of black for the owl's beak and eyes and the songbird's eye; white for the clouds, moon, and songbird's eye; two different yellows for the sun; gold for the owl's eyes and claws; and yellow for the songbird's beak and claws and the stars

BORDER

1½ yards (1.4 m) of a complementary print

BINDING

¼ yard (0.2 m) of brown

Notions & Such

Quilting Tool Kit (see page 11)

Appliqué patterns (page 136)

Pattern transfer materials and tools

4 yards (3.6 m) of medium-weight interfacing, 22 inches (55.9 cm) wide

4 yards (3.6 m) of paper-backed fusible webbing, 18 inches (45.7 cm) wide

All-purpose cotton-wrapped sewing thread to match all the appliqué fabrics

Invisible nylon thread for machine quilting

Medium-weight cotton batting

Finished Size

44 x 54 inches (111.8 x 137.2 cm)

Instructions

All of the seam allowances are ¼ inch (6 mm) wide.

Get Scrappy

1 Cut and seam the background yardage to make two 36½ x 46½-inch (92.7 x 118.1 cm) pieces. Back both pieces with the interfacing. Fusing the interfacing to the background fabric prevents the appliqués from puckering.

Way to Appliqué!

2 Enlarge the appliqué patterns and make templates for them. Trace them onto the paper side of the paper-backed fusible webbing, flipping the templates as needed. Fuse the shapes to the wrong side of the appliqué fabric, and cut them out. Remember, the shape that you trace onto the paper side of the webbing needs to be the reverse of what you want on the quilt top.

3 Fuse the appliqué shapes to the backgrounds, working on one side at a time. Start by positioning the bottom edge of the tree limb 14 inches (35.6 cm) from the bottom edge of the background. Use this as a guide for the other shapes. Make sure no shape—except the tree limb—touches the edge of the background. This ensures that the edges of the shapes won't get caught in a seam allowance.

4 Set your sewing machine for fairly wide zigzag stitches and a short stitch length. Your goal is to lay down stitching that isn't quite a satin stitch, but close. Appliqué each piece around the edges, changing thread colors as you work so that the thread and material always match.

Sew It Up

5 Cut the border fabric into long strips that are 4½ inches (11.4 cm) wide. You'll need 4 strips that are 36½ inches (92.7 cm) long and 4 more strips 54½ inches (138.4 cm) long.

6 Sew the short border strips to the top and bottom of the quilt, cut off any excess at the ends, and then sew the long borders to the sides. Be sure to keep your seam allowance consistent.

7 Stack and baste the quilt layers together. If you need to fudge a bit to get the edges of the quilt to line up, try easing the fabric in the middle of the quilt, rather than at the edges. You don't want one side of the border to be much shorter than the other edges.

8 Free-motion quilt the layers, using invisible nylon thread in the bobbin and the needle. It's sometimes necessary to loosen the tension of both the bobbin and the top thread when using invisible nylon thread.

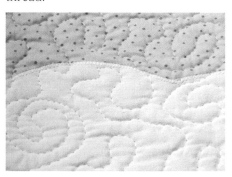

It's a Wrap

9 Bind the quilt with your desired method. Jude cut 1¼-inch-wide (3.2 cm) strips along the fabric length and used the single-fold binding technique.

BEHIND THE SEAMS WITH
xxxxxxxxxxxxxxxxxxxxx

Jude Stuecker

EARLIEST MEMORY: Looking up at my great-grandmother as she handed me a red M&M.

EARLIEST SEWING INFLUENCE: Karen Pritchett came to stay with my family on her tour with a puppetry caravan when I was nine years old. She is the reason I became a fiber artist.

MY STUDIO LOOKS LIKE: Almost everything I've ever loved in one room.

Inspire Me!

For something a little more on the cuddly side,
pick the rabbit and raccoon duo.

Fly Away Home

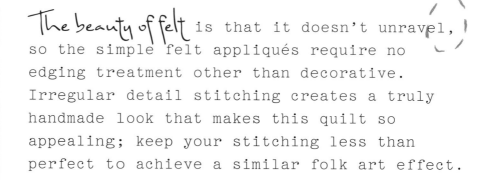

Julie Knoblock

The beauty of felt is that it doesn't unravel, so the simple felt appliqués require no edging treatment other than decorative. Irregular detail stitching creates a truly handmade look that makes this quilt so appealing; keep your stitching less than perfect to achieve a similar folk art effect.

Fabric

All fabric is cotton, 44 inches (111.8 cm) wide.

QUILT TOP AND BACKING
  1¾ yards (1.6 m) of cream cotton

APPLIQUÉS
  21 x 18½ inches (53.3 x 47 cm) of dull gold cotton for the tree
  10 x 13 inches (25.4 x 33 cm) of dark brown felt* for the tree
  8 x 9½ inches (20.3 x 24.1 cm) of lemon yellow cotton for the heart
  14 x 13 inches (35.6 x 33 cm) of teal cotton for the bird
  12¾ x 10¾ inches (32.4 x 27.3 cm) of cream felt* for the bird
  8-inch (20.3 cm) square of dark yellow felt* for the ovals

BORDER
  1 yard (0.9 m) of maroon cotton

* Choose a sturdy, thick felt. Found at fabric shops, this type is often sold off the bolt rather than as small squares. Craft felt may fall apart or rip easily when stitched.

Notions & Such

Quilting Tool Kit (see page 11)

Pattern transfer materials and tools

1⅛ yards (1 m) of fusible interfacing, 22 inches (55.9 cm) wide

Low-loft cotton batting

Embroidery needle with large eye

All-purpose cotton-wrapped sewing thread: cream, dark yellow, maroon, and teal

Skein each of embroidery floss**: dark brown, dark yellow, red, and teal

**Use three strands when embroidering.

Finished Size

32 x 39 inches (81.3 x 99 cm)

figure 1

Cutting Chart

Fabric	Quantity to cut	Size
Cream	(1)	29" x 36" (73.7 x 91.5 cm) for the quilt top
	(1)	32¾" x 39¾" (83.2 x 101 cm) for the backing
Maroon	(2)	2¼" x 36" (5.7 x 91.5 cm) for the border strips
	(2)	2¼" x 32" (5.7 x 81.3 cm) for the border strips
	Cut as desired for the binding	

Instructions

All of the seam allowances are ⅜ inch (1 cm) wide.

Get Scrappy

1 Cut the quilt top and the backing from the cream cotton fabric (see the cutting chart).

2 Refer to the whole quilt template (see figure 1) throughout these instructions. Enlarge the appliqué patterns. Apply interfacing to the back of the appliqué fabric and then trace and cut out the shapes.

Way to Appliqué!

3 Set your sewing machine for a straight stitch, and load it with the cream-colored sewing thread. Pin the rounded background shapes to the quilt top. Sew around the raw edges of the teal shape four or five times. Don't worry about making the stitching lines perfect. In fact, keep them a little messy for a charming folk art effect. Switch to teal sewing thread and sew around the dull gold and yellow shapes.

4 Pin the felt ovals to the quilt top. Machine sew them to the quilt top with matching thread and a line of straight stitching.

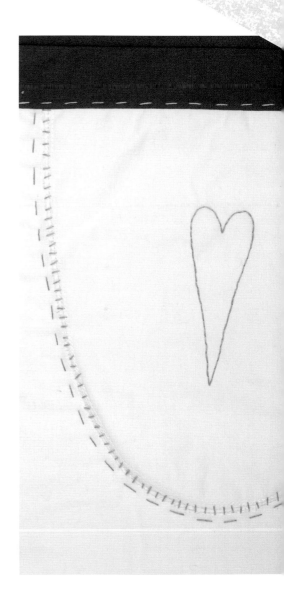

Embroider This!

5 Embroider the bird's outline with backstitches and dark brown floss. Pin the embroidered felt circle to the teal shape. Use the teal floss and blanket stitches to attach the felt circle to the fabric. Machine sew the tree trunk to the quilt top with matching sewing thread.

6 Backstitch the heart and treetops using dark yellow for the heart and red for the spirals. Use the teal floss to embroider small cross-stitches on the teal fabric around the bird, and use dark yellow floss to make straight stitches somewhat perpendicular to the edges of the yellow shape for the heart.

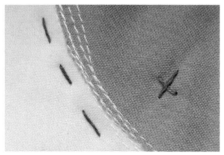

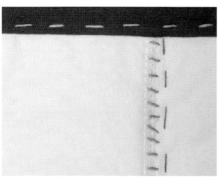

Sew It Up

7 Sew the longer border pieces to the lengthwise edges of the top, using matching thread. Press the seam allowances toward the border. Take care not to iron directly on any of the felt. Sew the end border pieces to the quilt top, and press the seam allowances outward.

8 Stack and baste the quilt layers together.

9 Use the teal floss to hand quilt three or so wavy rows of uneven running stitches just outside the perimeter of the dull gold fabric shape. Using the same color, hand quilt a row outside the yellow fabric shape. Switch to red floss and hand quilt one row outside the teal fabric shape. Load the sewing machine with cream sewing thread, and straight stitch closely just outside the ovals. Hand quilt just along the inner edge of the border with the dark yellow floss.

It's a Wrap

10 Bind the quilt with your desired method. Julie cut 3-inch-wide (7.6 cm) strips and used the double-layer binding technique with a ⅜-inch (1 cm) seam allowance and mitered corners.

Snippet

You don't need perfection for a folk art effect. Nevertheless, it's best to position all backstitching and knots (for the beginning and end of each line of stitching) in the seam allowance areas. To avoid drag lines (small diagonal folds) in the fabric, make the first line of stitching closest to the appliqué and make each new line a bit farther out. Basting first also helps.

Inspire Me!

Give your quilt a little western charm with a cowboy hat and trusty steed.

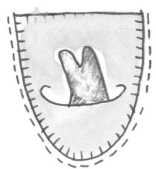

BEHIND THE SEAMS WITH

×××××××××××××××××××

Julie Knoblock

SEE MORE OF MY STUFF AT: www.julieknoblock.com or julieknoblock.blogspot.com

FIRST SEWING PROJECT: I desperately wanted to make a family of miniature fabric people I saw in a craft book. They were so small and fiddly that I convinced Mum to make them all for me once I gave up.

ONE WORD THAT BEST DESCRIBES YOUR ARTISTIC STYLE: Naïve.

WHAT IS YOUR FAVORITE PART OF QUILTING? The very last stitch.

Peekaboo

Carly Schwerdt

Besides having fun interactive elements, this quilt is also quite forgiving, so don't get too caught up in placing your fabric pieces in the same positions shown on Carly's quilt. Randomly cut and sew, and you can finish this piece in an afternoon.

Fabric

All fabric is cotton, 44 inches (111.8 cm) wide.

QUILT TOP
White fat quarter for transfer prints (or fabric images)
15 fat quarters of prints and solids for the pieced strips and flaps: brown, dark blue, green, orange, and red

QUILT TOP SASHES AND BACKING
1¾ yards (1.6 m) of orange

BINDING
1 yard (0.9 m) of a print

Notions & Such

Quilting Tool Kit (see page 11)

Photo transfer paper

Pattern transfer materials and tools

40½-inch (102.9 cm) square of low-loft batting

3⅜ yards (3 m) of natural cotton cord

All-purpose, cotton-wrapped cream-colored sewing thread

Finished Size

33 inches (83.8 cm) in diameter

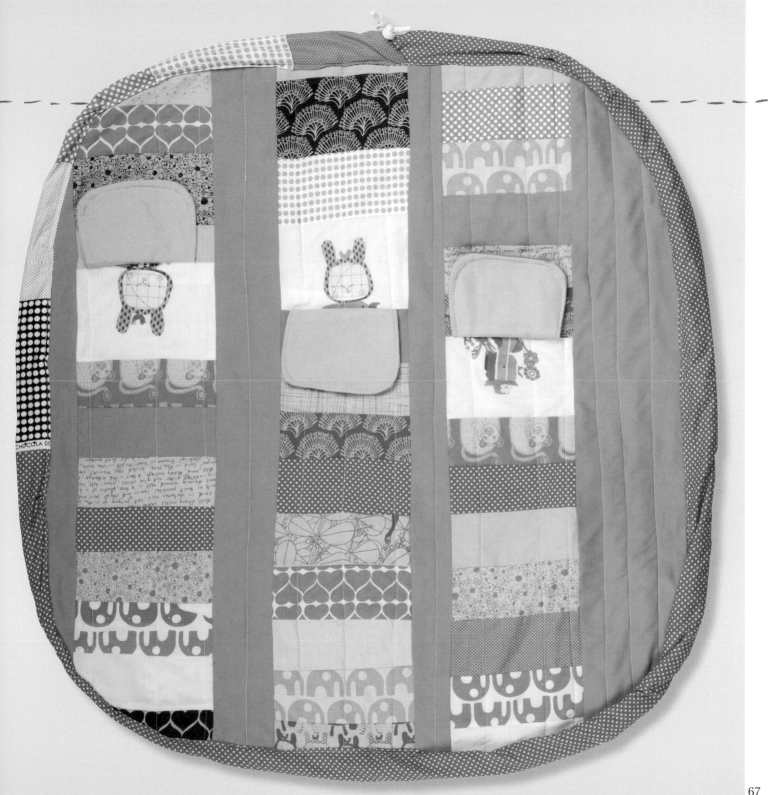

Instructions

All of the seam allowances are ¼ inch (6 mm) wide.

Get Scrappy

1 Cut four strips from the solid orange yardage, all 34 inches (86.4 cm) long and with widths ranging from 4 to 8 inches (10.2 to 20.3 cm).

2 Cut 40 to 50 pieces that are 8 inches (20.3 cm) wide and range in length from 4 to 8 inches (10.2 to 20.3 cm).

3 Use the photo transfer paper to print color images on the white cotton fabric or see the sidebar (page 70) for other peekaboo option ideas. Cut around the images to make three rectangles that are 8 inches (20.3 cm) wide and any length.

Sew It Up

4 To make the flaps, cut six fabric and three batting rectangles that measure 6 x 4½ inches (15.2 x 11.4 cm).

5 Hold two flap shapes right sides together, and place a batting shape on top. Sew them together, creating curves at the bottom corners and leaving the straight top edge open. Turn the flap right side out, and then sew through all layers along the curved edge. Make two more flaps.

6 Place a flap on top of each printed rectangle (or on your chosen fabric peekaboo image), both right side up. You want the straight, raw edge of each flap aligned with—and centered on—the upper edge of the white fabric. Baste them together.

7 Sew together the fabric pieces to make three patchwork strips that are all 8 inches (20.3 cm) wide. Position a peekaboo image rectangle in each strip. When joining a piece to a print rectangle, the upper edge of a flap will be caught in the seam line. Press all of the seam allowances toward the bottom of the strip. Your goal is to make strips that are 34 inches (86.4 cm) long.

8 Sew together the lengthwise edges of the pieced strips and sashes. Press down the seam allowances.

9 Stack the top, batting, and backing together. Trim the corners so your quilt is nice and rounded.

10 Quilt parallel to the long seams that join the patchwork and plain strips. Position these lines randomly so that some are closer together and others are farther apart. Make sure there are two quilted lines on every strip. Eventually, a flap will get in the way when you're quilting. Sew right up to the flap and then end the seam. Start quilting again directly on the other side of the flap.

It's a Wrap

11 Cut the binding fabric into bias strips, and attach them to the quilt with your desired method, starting in the middle at the quilt's top and overlapping the ends. For a clean finish, press both raw, short edges to the wrong side before you sew the ends in place. Don't sew the horizontal overlapped ends closed. If you run out of binding fabric, just continue to lengthen the binding with patchwork leftovers. Carly used the single-fold method, starting with a 6¼-inch-wide (15.9 cm) strip. She used a ⅜-inch (9.5 mm) seam allowance so that the finished binding on her quilt is 2¾ inches (7 cm) wide.

12 Pull the cord through the bias tape, and knot both ends to prevent them from slipping inside the binding.

BEHIND THE SEAMS WITH

XXXXXXXXXXXXXXXXXXX

Carly Schwerdt

SEE MORE OF MY STUFF AT: www.neststudio.typepad.com and www.umbrellaprints.typepad.com

DAY JOB: Mother, graphic designer, art teacher, store owner, and textile designer.

PLACE I GO FOR INSPIRATION: Spending time with my daughter and husband, reading blogs and Japanese craft books, and sketching in my millions of sketchbooks.

MY NEXT QUILTING PROJECT: A baby quilt large enough to fit a toddler bed and one to fit a single bed for my daughter... (I am used to making dolly quilts.)

Peekaboo images can be whatever you'd like baby to discover under the flaps. The possibilities are endless.
Try using:

◎ Bold appliqué images of familiar objects—a teddy, an apple, or a car, etc.—using felt

◎ Embroidery patterns

◎ Large fabric pattern images

◎ Photos of the baby's family*

◎ Your own artwork or an older sibling's drawings*

*You can accomplish this by transferring the image onto cotton.

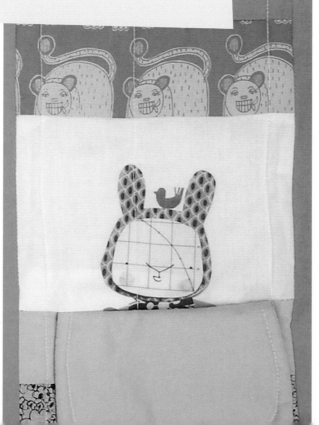

Monkey Business

The monkey tummy, eye, and nose patch appliqués are sewn on after the quilt has been assembled in a process dubbed appliquilting. The stitching you do to attach the shapes to the quilt top will also quilt the layers together in one simple step.

Laurraine Yuyama

Fabric

All of the fabric is 44 inches (111.8 cm) wide.

QUILT TOP

10½ x 12-inch (26.7 x 30.5 cm) pieces of 9 cotton prints for the monkey blocks

3½ x 12-inch (8.9 x 30.5 cm) pieces of 6 cotton prints for the short sashes

⅛ yard (0.1 m) of 6 cotton prints for the inner borders

½ yard (0.5 m) of 4 cotton prints for the outer borders and sashes

APPLIQUÉS

6 x 12-inch (15.2 x 30.5 cm) pieces of 8 cotton prints for the shirts

½ yard (0.5 m) of brown corduroy for the monkeys

½ yard (0.5 m) of cream cotton print for the ears, faces, and tummies

BACKING

2⅜ yards (2.1 m) of brown striped fabric

Notions & Such

Quilting Tool Kit (see page 11)

Appliqué and quilting patterns (page 132)

Pattern transfer materials and tools

Felt scraps: black for the eyes and a variety of colors for 24 buttons

Single-hole paper punch

Pinking shears (optional)

Chopstick or knitting needle

Embroidery needle

High-loft polyester batting

All-purpose cotton-wrapped sewing thread: dark brown, tan, and colors matched to the felt and shirts

Skein each of embroidery floss*: black, brown, and light gray

*Use six strands when embroidering.

Finished Size

49 x 54 inches (124.5 x 137.2 cm) after washing

Border Cutting Chart

Name of piece	Quantity to cut	Size
Outer border	(2)	55" x 7½" (139.7 x 19 cm)
	(2)	7½" x 46½" (19 x 118.1 cm)
Inner border	(2)	37½" x 2¾" (95.3 x 7 cm)
	(2)	2¾" x 46½" (7 x 118.1 cm)
Sash	(6)	3½" x 12" (8.9 x 30.5 cm)
	(2)	37½" x 3½" (95.3 x 8.9 cm)

figure 1

Appliqué Cutting Chart

Name of piece	Fabric	Quantity to cut
Shirt	8 prints	(16)
	Brown corduroy	(1)
Arm	Brown corduroy	(9)
		Flip and cut (9) more
Head	Brown corduroy	(9)
Ear	Brown corduroy	(18)
	Cream print	(18)
Tummy patch	Cream print	(2)
Nose patch	Cream print	(18)
Eye patch	Cream print	(18)
Eye	Black felt	(18)

Instructions

All of the seam allowances are ¼ inch (6 mm) wide unless otherwise noted.

Get Scrappy

1 Refer to the whole quilt template (see figure 1) throughout these instructions. Cut all of the pieces according to the border cutting chart. Some strips are longer than the fabric yardage, so sew together shorter pieces to create the longer borders.

Way to Appliqué!

2 Enlarge the appliqué patterns, and cut the fabric shapes as listed in the appliqué cutting chart. As you cut the shapes from corduroy, rotate the templates so that the fabric's surface texture travels in different directions. Use the hole punch to cut the eyes.

3 Arrange the pieces for the eye patch, nose patch, and shirt in matched pairs. Match each corduroy ear with a cream-colored one. Sew the pairs together wrong side out, leaving open the tops and bottoms of the shirts and the bottoms of the eye patches and ears. Cut a slit in one side of each nose and tummy patch (see figure 2). Using the chopstick or knitting needle, turn the pieces right side out. Press them.

4 Machine-embroider the nose and mouth on every nose appliqué, using thin, narrow satin stitches and the dark brown thread.

5 Attach the felt eyes to the eye patches with a horizontal straight stitch using the black embroidery floss and a vertical stitch with the light gray embroidery floss.

Building Blocks

6 Pin a monkey head, shirt, and arms on each block, tilting the heads in different directions. One block, which will be the center of the quilt, will feature a shirtless monkey. Use the corduroy body instead, and follow the same procedure for attaching the appliqués.

7 Lift a shirt away from the arms on one of the blocks. Sew along the outer edges of the arms using brown thread and dense, wide satin stitches. Fold in both sides of an ear so that the cream-colored print peeks out from the interior (see figure 3). Fold

another ear, and pin both under the head at different angles. Replace the shirt with the top edge tucked under the head. Sew around the head with the same stitch and thread. Sew the appliqués to the rest of the blocks.

8 Cut 24 felt buttons in a variety of shapes. Tack three to each shirt with the brown embroidery floss. Sew around the edge of each button with straight stitches and matching thread.

9 Piece three monkey blocks, side by side, with a short sash between each one. Make two more rows of monkey blocks and short sashes. Sew the rows together with a longer sash between each one.

10 Sew the shorter inner border strips to the top and bottom. Next, add a longer inner border to each side. Sew the shorter outer borders to the sides. Finally, add the longer outer borders to the top and bottom.

11 Cut and sew the backing to a suitable shape and size.

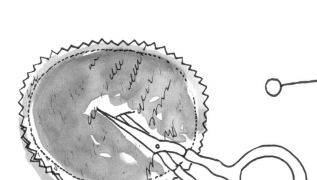

figure 2

figure 3

Sew It Up

12 Following the quick-turn method (page 28), place the backing face up on top of the batting and center the quilt top facedown on top. Pin and sew around the edge using a ½-inch (1.3 cm) seam allowance and leaving a 10-inch (25.4 cm) opening at the bottom. Cut off the excess batting and backing, and trim across the corners. Turn the quilt right side out. Use the chopstick to punch out the corners, and hand sew the opening closed with appliqué stitches.

13 Baste the layers together, and machine quilt along all of the seam lines using the tan thread in the needle and brown thread in the bobbin.

14 Set the sewing machine for blanket stitches, and sew down the sides of the shirts using a different color thread for each one. Switch to dark brown thread and straight stitches, and sew closely around the outside edges of the arms and the heads.

15 Pin the tummy, eye, and nose patches to the monkeys, tilting the faces to match the angle of the ears. Sew around them with tan thread and machine blanket stitches. Don't sew over the felt eyes.

16 Enlarge the quilting templates on page 132, and make paper templates. Trace the shapes on the quilt top: bananas on one outer border, circles on another, numbers on a third, and flowers on the fourth. Quilt the shapes with matching thread.

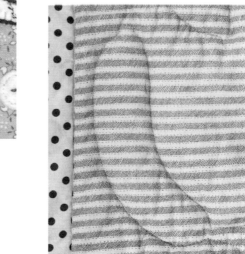

Inspire Me!

If monkeys just don't do it for you, use the same design idea to create a quilt chock full-o-bunnies.

78

Giddyup, Sea Horse

If your favored method for making fabric applique shapes doesn't call for freezer paper, now is the time to give this household product a whirl. Freezer-paper patterns are great for making detailed fabric silhouettes, especially sea horses.

Glynis Cotton

Fabric

All fabric is cotton, 44 inches (111.8 cm) wide.

QUILT TOP
 1½ yards (1.4 m) of a pale pink solid

APPLIQUÉS
 ½ yard (0.5 m) each of two different green prints

QUILT BACKING
 2 yards (1.8 m) of one of the prints

Notions & Such

Quilting Tool Kit (see page 11)

Appliqué pattern (page 138)

Freezer paper

Fine-tip, indelible ink felt marking pen

Medium-loft cotton batting

All-purpose cotton-wrapped light pink sewing thread

Pattern transfer materials and tools

Finished Size

48 x 36 inches (121.9 x 91.4 cm)

Instructions

All of the seam allowances are ¼ inch (6 mm) wide.

Get Scrappy

1 Cut or seam the quilt top yardage to 48 x 36 inches (121.9 x 91.4 cm).

2 Copy the sea horse appliqué pattern, and then use the marking pen to trace the shape three times on the matte side of the freezer paper. Flip the paper over and trace the shape again to make five more templates on the shiny side of the freezer paper. Cut the sea horses from the paper.

Way to Appliqué!

3 Pin four of the sea horses, matte side down, on the wrong side of one of the appliqué prints. Only use a few pins. Pin the rest of the sea horses on the other fabric.

4 Cut the sea horses from the fabric, including a ¼-inch (6 mm) fabric seam allowance beyond the paper edges, around the perimeter of every shape. Clip through the seam allowance of each appliqué (figure 1). Space the clips every ¼ inch (6 mm)—closer around sharp turns and inside inner corners.

figure 1

5 Fold the seam allowances over the freezer paper, and iron them down so that they stick to the shiny side.

Note: You may need a little steam to get the freezer paper to stick. Be careful: if the paper gets too wet it won't adhere to the fabric.

6 Pin the sea horses, right side up, on the quilt top. Remove the freezer paper, one at a time, and then pin each shape back on the quilt top with the seam allowances tucked underneath.

7 Machine sew around the perimeter of each sea horse with straight stitches and the matching light pink thread.

Sew It Up

8 Pin the quilt layers together. Cut the backing so that it extends 2 inches (5 cm) beyond each edge of the quilt top.

9 Quilt diagonal lines 3 inches (7.6 cm) apart over the entire top.

It's a Wrap

10 Wrap the backing around the edges of the layers, to the front of the quilt. Fold under the backing's raw edge to create a 1-inch (2.5 cm) border on the quilt top. Pin down the border, and fold all of the corners to make miters.

11 Sew around the border as close to the edges as possible. Sew diagonal lines along each mitered corner.

Snippet

Don't lose your place when you're stitching around a tight corner: Stop at the corner with the needle down through the fabric layers. Lift the presser foot and pivot the quilt top. When the new edge is aligned for stitching, drop the presser foot and continue stitching.

Inspire Me!

In the mood for something a little different? Create a different kind of herd with snazzy snails.

BEHIND THE SEAMS WITH

Glynis Cotton

SEE MORE OF MY STUFF AT: www.dandelionquilts.com.

MOST TREASURED BABY BLANKET: My grandmother made quilts for my sister and me out of a bright orange and red paisley '70s fabric. She used her old panty hose as batting.

MY NEXT QUILTING PROJECT: My dream project is to appliqué the silhouette of a gothic, Victorian house on a king-sized quilt.

LEAST FAVORITE CHILDHOOD NICKNAME: Glynis the menace

Lemongrass

This quilt has 16 unique blocks. Complicated? Not at all. The pattern is based on a simple log cabin design—without the usual demand for precision. The quilting features freeform concentric circles, a visually pleasing accent to the freeform rectangles.

Laura Ducommun

Fabric

All of the fabric is cotton, 44 inches (111.8 cm) wide.

QUILT TOP AND BINDING
- 1½ yards (1.4 m) of yellow-and-white polka dot for the block centers
- 1 yard (0.9 m) of a green-and-yellow floral for the blocks
- ¾ yard (0.7 m) of a multi-colored stripe
- 1½ yards (1.4 m) of white for the sashes

BACKING
- 2 yards (1.8 m) of grass-green

Notions & Such

Quilting Tool Kit (see page 11)

Low-loft batting

All-purpose cotton-wrapped white sewing thread

White cotton quilting thread

Finished Size

40 x 52 inches (101.6 x 132.1 cm)

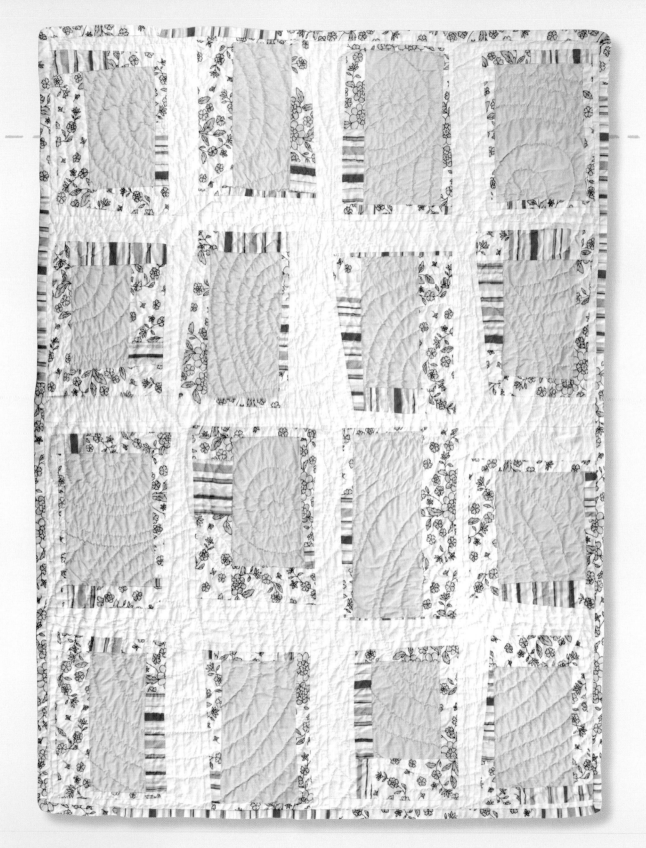

Instructions

The seam allowances are ¼ inch (6 mm) wide, except as noted.

Get Scrappy

1 Cut 16 rectangles from the block center fabric. Make a variety of sizes: some short and fat and others long and thin, but none more than 12 x 7 inches (30.5 x 17.8 cm).

Note: The more you vary the size of the center block, the more unique this quilt will be.

2 Cut three-quarters of the floral fabric and all of the striped yardage into pieces, with widths ranging from 1½ to 5 inches (3.8 to 12.7 cm) and random lengths ranging from 3 to 10 inches (7.6 to 25.4 cm).

3 Sort the floral and striped pieces into groups of similar widths. Sew the pieces in each group together, alternating the florals and stripes, to make lengths no longer than 22 inches (55.9 cm). This length is just a guide; you can work with long strips and cut off what you need as you go along. Trim the lengthwise edges so they're straight.

4 Cut the white yardage into strips ranging from 1½ to 5 inches (3.8 to 12.7 cm) wide and no more than 14 inches (35.6 cm) long.

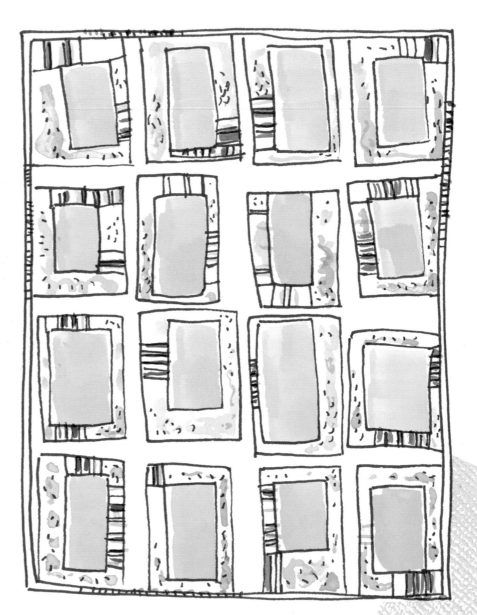

figure 1

Building Blocks

5 Refer to the whole quilt template (see figure 1) throughout the rest of these instructions. Select four pieced strips that all have different widths. Sew one of the strips to an edge of a yellow square, with the right sides together, and cut off the excess pieced length at the end of the seam. Attach the rest of the strips to a different edge, working your way around the growing block (see figure 2).

6 Cut random angles around the outer edges of the block. Add strips around the remaining yellow blocks, and cut random angles on them.

7 Attach white fabric strips to the edge of all the blocks until each one is 11 x 14 inches (27.9 x 35.6 cm). To be safe, you can make the blocks bigger and cut them down once all the strips have been added.

8 Piece together all of the blocks, using ½-inch (1.3 cm) seam allowances.

Sew It Up

9 Stack and baste the quilt layers together.

10 Quilt random circles ½ to 1 inch (1.3 to 2.5 cm) apart, using the white quilting thread. Don't worry about each line being perfectly straight—wobbly lines make the quilt more interesting.

figure 2

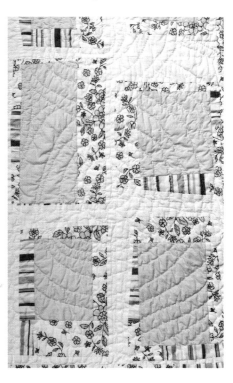

It's a Wrap

11 Bind your quilt with your desired method. Laura pieced floral and stripe leftovers to make a 2 ½-inch-wide (6.4 cm) binding strip. She used the double-fold binding technique, ¼-inch (6 mm) seam allowances, and mitered corners.

Snippet

The floral yardage is enough fabric to let you play around with each block. If a particular block doesn't turn out, just start again. You'll have enough strips to complete the squares, and you can cut more if needed.

BEHIND THE SEAMS WITH
x x x x x x x x x x x x x x x x x x x
Laura Ducommun

MOST TREASURED BABY BLANKET: It wasn't a baby blanket, but my aunt made me a "kitty quilt" in high school. It is falling apart now, but I still love it. My husband recently asked my aunt to make me a new "kitty quilt." She just completed it, and it's amazing.

MY FIRST BABY WORD: "No!" (Can you tell that I'm stubborn?)

WHEN I GROW UP: I wanted to be an astronaut… or a ballet dancer… or a beautician… or a writer… I am still trying to figure it out!

Over the Orchard

A flock of appliquéd birds soar over this quaint orchard scene. Detailed embroidery, raw-edged appliqué, and free-motion quilting create a sense of motion. A clever variation lets you swap out the appliqués to "city-fy" the quilt for the modern urban baby.

Kajsa Wikman

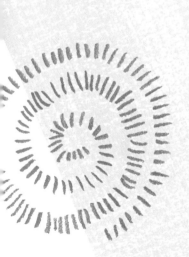

89

Fabric

All fabric is 44 inches (111.8 cm) wide.

QUILT TOP BACKGROUND
  1½ yards (1.4 m) of natural-colored linen

OUTER BORDER, HORIZONTAL STRIPS, APPLIQUÉS, AND BACKING
  ½ yard (0.5 m) each of at least six light-colored cottons: light orange, light teal or blue, and off-white
  ½ yard (0.5 m) each of at least six dark-colored cottons: grayish blue, orange, and teal

INNER BORDER AND TREE TRUNK APPLIQUÉS
  ¼ yard (0.3 m) each of two different cottons: dark brown and turquoise

BINDING AND TREETOP APPLIQUÉS
  ¼ yard (0.3 m) of orange cotton (or enough scraps of several orange cottons)

Notions & Such

Quilting Tool Kit (see page 11)

Appliqué patterns (page 137)

Pattern transfer materials and tools

Paper-backed fusible webbing, 18 inches (45.7 cm) wide

Embroidery needle

Embroidery hoop

Low-loft cotton or polyester batting

All-purpose cotton-wrapped off-white sewing thread

Cotton machine embroidery thread: black and off-white

Skein each of embroidery floss: black and teal

Finished Size

36 x 40 inches (91.4 x 101.6 cm)

Cutting Chart

Fabric color	Name of piece	Quantity to cut	Size
Grayish blue, light orange, light teal or blue, off-white, orange, and teal	A	(10) of each color to total of (60)	3½" (8.9 cm) square
	B	(25)	1½" x varying lengths of 2" to 6½" (3.8 x 5 to 16.5 cm)
Natural-colored linen	C	(1)	28" x 6¾" (71.1 x 17.2 cm)
	D	(1)	28" x 7¼" (71.1 x 18.4 cm)
	E	(2)	28" x 7¾" (71.1 x 19.7 cm)
Dark brown and turquoise	G	(15)	1½" x varying lengths of 5" to 15" (3.8 x 12.7 to 38.1 cm)

Instructions

All of the seam allowances are ¼ inch (6 mm) wide.

Get Scrappy

1 Cut the fabric for the quilt top as detailed in the cutting chart. If you're using different fabric colors than what Kajsa selected, reference the horizontal strips on the background as you pick colors for your appliqués. It'll help you achieve a pleasing balance of colors throughout the quilt top.

2 Sew together enough of the light- and dark-colored rectangles (B)—joining them at the short ends—to make three 28-inch-long (71.1 cm) strips. Press all of the seam allowances to one side, as preferred.

3 Sew the linen rectangles (C, D, and E) and the pieced horizontal strips together along the lengthwise edges, as shown in figure 1. Press the seam allowances to the linen sides.

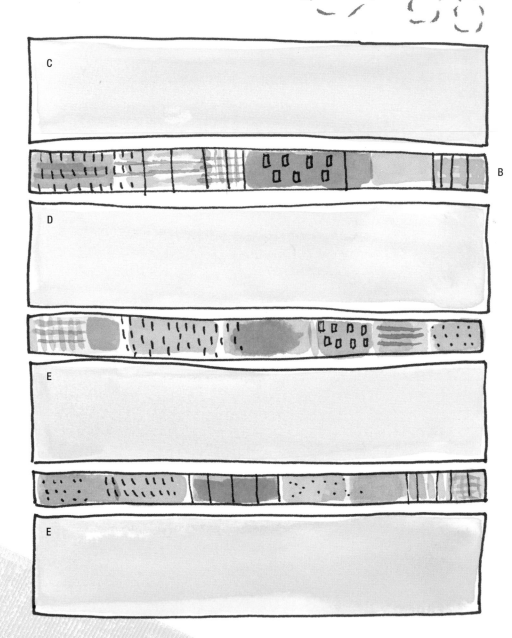

figure 1

Way to Appliqué!

4 Enlarge and make templates for the appliqués. Flip them over, so that the shapes are reversed, and trace them onto the paper-backed side of the fusible webbing. Cut the shapes from the fusible webbing, adding a ¼-inch (6 mm) seam allowance to all of the edges. Press the webbing to the wrong side of the appliqué fabrics and then cut them out. Transfer the #1 design lines to the front of the house appliqué.

5 Fuse all of the appliqué pieces on the quilt top background except bird #1. Press it onto an off-white square, and set this aside. Machine-sew around the edges of all of the shapes with straight stitches and the black machine embroidery thread. Machine-embroider the bird beaks and legs with straight stitches.

Note: If your machine has an appliqué foot, use this to sew around the fabric shapes. The open (or transparent) toe on the foot makes it easier to see where to stitch.

6 Hand embroider the appliqués: Use three strands of the teal floss to create running stitches for the steam coming out of the chimney and back stitches for the house number. Switch to four strands of the black floss and work the pear's stem with back stitches, then make a dot at the bottom of the stem.

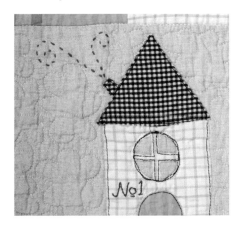

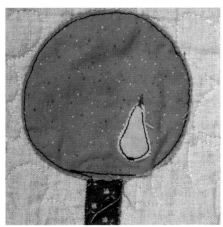

Sew It Up

7 Sew together the short ends of the dark brown and turquoise rectangles (G), alternating the colors, to make a 62-inch-long (157.5 cm) strip. Sew one long side to an edge of the quilt top. Cut off the excess strip, and press the seam allowances toward the borders. Attach the rest of this inner border around the remaining sides of the quilt.

Note: Plan your outer border color scheme by arranging the separate squares (A) around the perimeter of the assembled quilt top. Kajsa alternated light- and dark-colored squares.

8 Sew together 10 squares (A) for the top outer border. Sew this length to the quilt top, and press the seam allowances toward the linen. Assemble and join a border to the bottom of the quilt top. Make and attach the side borders last, using the off-white bird-appliqué square in the upper right corner.

9 Sew together the remaining squares and rectangles (A, B, and G)—and any other leftover yardage—to compose the backing.

10 Stack and baste the quilt layers together.

11 Load your sewing machine with the off-white embroidery thread, and adjust the machine for free-motion quilting. Stitch cloud shapes through the layers, starting from the middle of the quilt. Stitch a few times in place to secure the thread at start and finish of each line of quilting. Quilt the horizontal stripes and borders along the seam lines.

It's a Wrap

12 Bind the quilt with your desired method. Kajsa cut 1-inch-wide (2.5 cm) strips along the length of the same orange fabric that she used for the tree appliqués. She attached the length using the single-fold binding technique.

Snippet

Your quilt is a celebration, so think about embroidering (or printing with indelible ink) your name and the date of completion on one of the backing squares. Future generations will cherish this information.

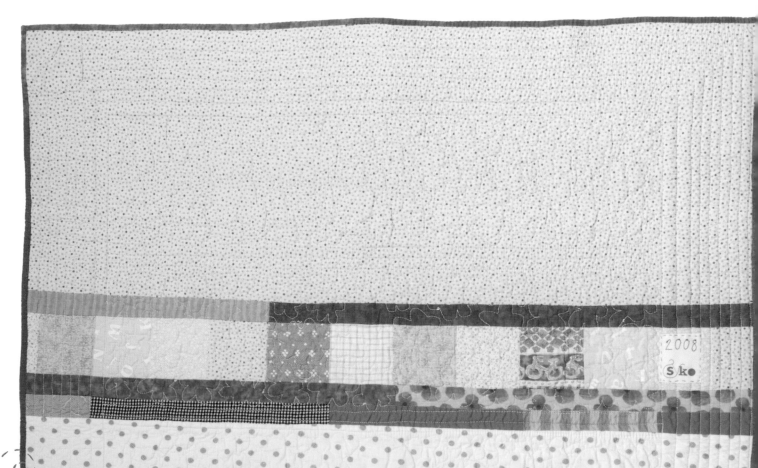

Inspire Me!

Create a city landscape by using these endearing apartment building and fir tree appliqués.

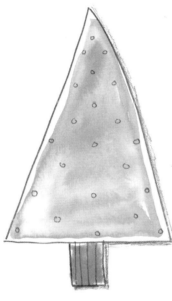

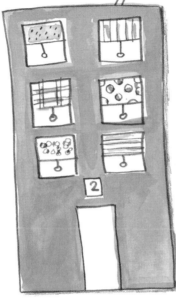

BEHIND THE SEAMS WITH

xxxxxxxxxxxx xx x x xxxxx

Kajsa Wikman

SEE MORE OF MY STUFF AT: www.syko.fi

EARLIEST SEWING INSTRUCTOR/INFLUENCE: My mum has always been creating, and she's a great inspiration. We always call each other when a new craft project is started, which is almost daily!

WHAT TIME OF DAY DO YOU FIND MOST CONDUCIVE TO CRAFTING? Noon. But I get the best ideas in the shower.

WHAT IS YOUR FAVORITE PART OF QUILTING? The rush of a new idea and dragging out a fair amount of fabrics from the shelves; in other words, making a mess!

Stair-Crazy

Update one of the most timeless beginner quilt designs, the basic stair step, with boisterous redwork kittens at play. By adding a tutu or baseball bat, individual kitties can be accessorized to reflect an older sibling's interests.

Dorie
Blaisdell
Schwarz

Fabric

All fabric is cotton.

QUILT TOP
- 1½ yards (1.4 m) of white, 36 inches (91.4 cm) wide
- 3 x 19-inch (7.6 x 48.3 cm) piece of blue basketweave (A)
- ½ yard (0.5 m) each of two prints: red dots (D) and blue floral (E), 36 inches (91.4 cm) wide
- ¼ yard (0.3 m) each of four prints: red floral (B), red circle (C), gingham (F), and blue medallions (G), 36 inches (91.4 cm) wide
- 3 x 11½-inch (7.6 cm x 29.2 cm) piece of red floral print (H)

QUILT BACKING
- 1¾ yards (1.6 m) of white, 90 inches (228 cm) wide

BINDING
- ½ yard (0.5 m) of red floral, 36 inches (91 cm) wide

Notions & Such

Quilting Tool Kit (see page 11)

Embroidery patterns (page 135)

Embroidery needle and hoop

Low-loft cotton batting

All-purpose cotton-wrapped white sewing thread

Pattern transfer materials and tools

2 skeins of red embroidery floss*

*Use three strands when embroidering.

Finished Size

56 x 40 inches (142.2 x 101.6 cm)

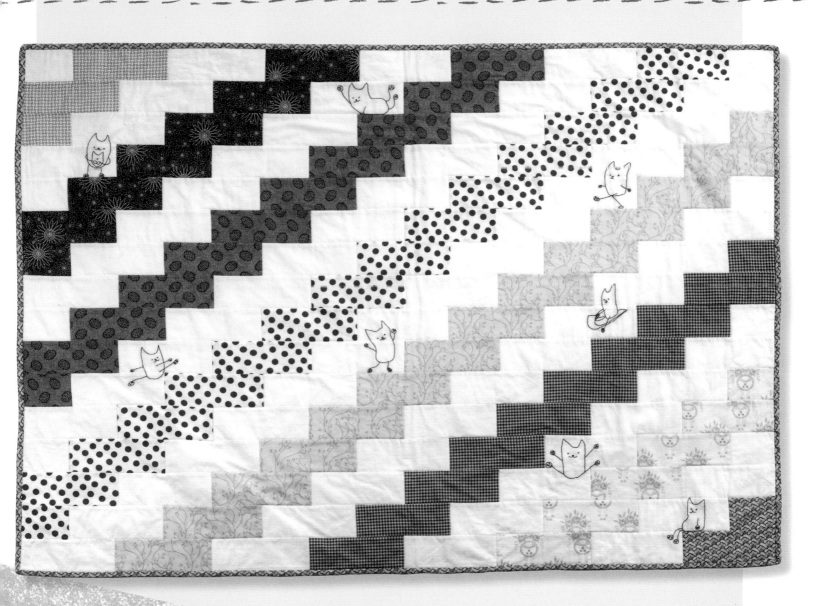

Cutting Chart

Fabric	Quantity to cut to 3" x 4" (7.6 x 10.2 cm)	Quantity to cut to 3" x 7½" (7.6 x 19 cm)
White	(8)	(60)
Red floral (H)	(1)	(1)
Blue medallions (G)	(1)	(5)
Gingham (F)	(1)	(9)
Blue floral (E)	(1)	(13)
Red dots (D)	(1)	(14)
Red circles (C)	(1)	(10)
Red floral (B)	(1)	(6)
Blue basketweave (A)	(1)	(2)

Instructions

All of the seam allowances are ¼ inch (6 mm) wide.

Get Scrappy

1 Refer to the whole quilt illustration (see figure 1) throughout these instructions. Cut the fabric according to the cutting chart.

2 Join one edge of a white-fabric square to a blue-basketweave rectangle (A) by pinning them right sides together along the short edge and sewing with a straight stitch and white sewing thread. Open the squares along the seam line. For this and all seams on the quilt top, press the seam allowances toward the darker fabric.

3 Sew a white rectangle to the opposite side of the joined pair. Continue adding blocks to the row by sewing each new one to the remaining side of the block you just added. Follow the first line (or row) of figure 1 to determine the order of the colors.

4 When you've finished the first row, set it aside and start the second. Continue this way until you've made 16 rows. At this point, all of the rows are separate.

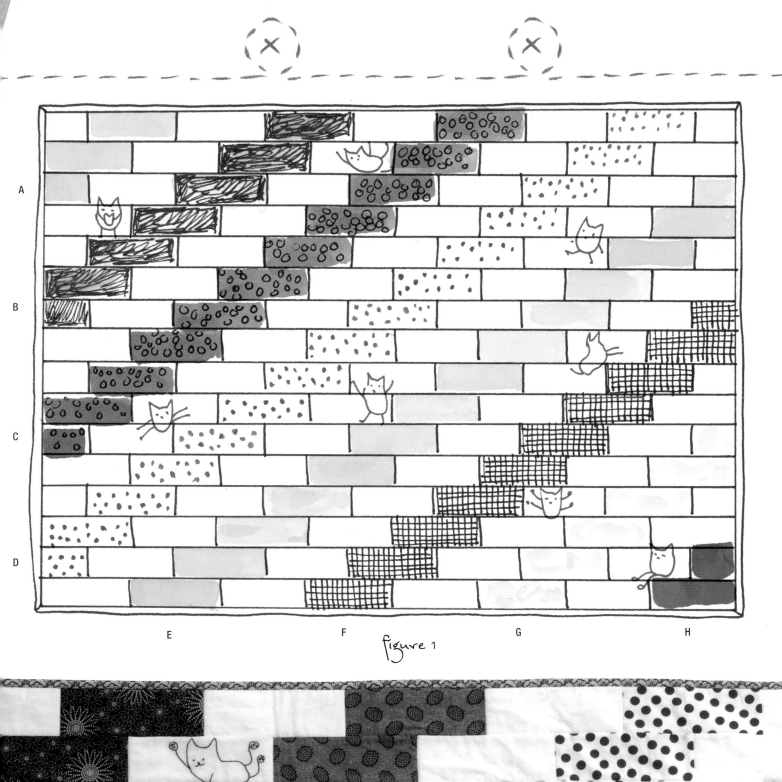

figure 1

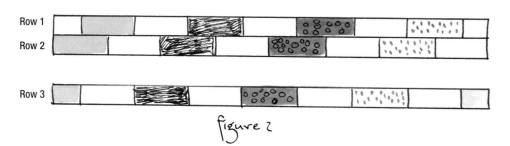

Row 1
Row 2

Row 3

figure 2

5 Sew the bottom of row 1 to the top of row 2. Sew all of the rows with right sides together, matching the ends and the edges of one row's blocks to the middle of the next row's blocks (see figure 2). Open the rows and press the seam allowances toward the bottom of the quilt. Join the rest of the rows to make the quilt top.

Embroider This!

6 Transfer the embroidery patterns onto the quilt top, using figure 1 as a placement guide. Embroider the design lines with the red embroidery floss. Use backstitches for the lines, a small backstitch for each eye on the baby cat, and French knots for all the rest of the eyes.

Note: Dorie likes to trace her embroidery patterns with a pencil that has a sharp point because the lines are more precise.

Sew It Up

7 Stack and baste the quilt layers together. Dorie recommends that you trim the batting and backing ¼ inch (6 mm) larger than the quilt top. She does this because she wants a ½-inch-wide (1.3 cm) finished binding

but doesn't want to take a ½-inch (1.3 cm) seam allowance around the quilt top. With one seam, she sews on the binding using a ¼-inch (6 mm) seam allowance for the top and ½ inch (1.3 cm) for the batting and backing. The extra ¼ inch (6 mm) of batting and backing fill out the binding when it's wrapped to the underside. This quilt doesn't have an outer border, so keeping the narrower seam allowance on the top maintains the proportions of the bricks.

8 Quilt diagonal zigzag lines by following the zigzags created by the outer edges of the colored pieces. You won't sew through any embroidery by quilting in this manner.

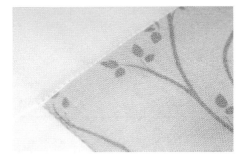

It's a Wrap

9 Bind the quilt with your desired method. Dorie cut 2½-inch-wide (6.4 cm) strips along the width of her binding fabric. She used the double-fold binding technique, ½-inch (1.3 cm) seam allowances, and mitered corners.

Snippet
You can eliminate fabric wrinkles (drag lines) along the quilting lines by replacing the standard presser foot on your sewing machine with a walking foot.

Inspire Me!

Not a cat person? Swap 'em out for these little forest creatures—they're just as energetic as their feline friends!

Skippy, the Elephant

The straight grid lines, created by first drawing lines on the fabric with a chalk marker, create a nice contrasting backdrop for the bold, raw-edged elephant appliqué. You can customize this quilt easily with a different animal, but with this design, the bigger the appliqué shape, the better.

Erin Harris

Fabric

All of the fabric is cotton, 44 inches (111.8 cm) wide.

QUILT TOP
  1¾ yards (1.6 m) of gray

APPLIQUÉS
  ¾ yard (0.7 m) of aqua-brown-gray plaid for the elephant body
  ½ yard (0.5 m) of aqua print for the ear
  3-inch (7.6 cm) square of brown print for the eye

BACKING
  1¾ yards (1.6 m) of brown
  10 to 12 pieces, each at least 4 inches (10.2 cm) wide and long: aqua, brown, and gray prints

BINDING
  ¼ yard (0.2 m) of aqua print

Notions & Such

Quilting Tool Kit (see page 11)

Appliqué pattern (page 138)

Pattern transfer materials and tools of choice

3 yards (2.7 m) of paper-backed fusible webbing, 18 inches (45.7 cm) wide

All-purpose cotton-wrapped sewing thread: brown and gray

Low-loft cotton batting

Finished Size

54 x 37 inches (137.2 x 94 cm)

Instructions

All of the seam allowances are ¼ inch (6 mm) wide.

Get Scrappy

1. Cut the gray fabric to make a 56 x 39-inch (142.2 x 99.1 cm) rectangle for the quilt top's background.

Way to Appliqué!

2. Enlarge the appliqué patterns, flip them over, and trace them onto the paper side of the paper-backed fusible webbing. Fuse the shapes to the wrong side of the appliqué fabrics, and cut them out. You may need to use two pieces of webbing for the elephant. In this case, cut them to 40 x 18 inches (101.6 x 45.7 cm) and 40 x 9 inches (101.6 x 22.9 cm). Fuse these to the wrong side of the plaid fabric, butting the two edges so they meet along the longer side but don't overlap. Transfer the ear and eye placement marks to the fabric appliqué shapes.

3. Place the elephant on the quilt top, aligning the left side and the bottom of the elephant body ⅛ inch (3 mm) from the left bottom corner of the gray background fabric. Fuse it in place by starting in the bottom corner and working out and up. Take care that the fabrics don't pucker.

4. Fuse the ear and the eye in place.

5. Sew around the appliqué shapes ⅛ inch (3 mm) from all of the fabric edges, using the brown thread and straight stitches. To make this easier, always stop sewing with your needle in the down position and pivot your fabric at the corners and on curves as necessary.

BEHIND THE SEAMS WITH

x x x x x x x x x x x x x x x

Erin Harris

SEE MORE OF MY STUFF AT: houseonhillroad.com

MOST TREASURED BABY BLANKET: I had five pink receiving blankets that had to be counted every night when I went to bed. If any were missing, my mom would take the bottom one and put it on top until she got to five.

FAVORITE TUNES TO QUILT TO: Garden State soundtrack and Craftsanity podcasts

MOST CHALLENGING THING ABOUT QUILTING: Trusting my gut and following my instincts. When I don't do that, I really am not happy with the end result.

Sew It Up

6 Cut the brown fabric for the backing into two shapes: 42 inches (106.7 cm) square and 42 x 12 inches (106.7 x 30.5 cm).

7 Using figure 1 as a guide, cut all of the prints to 4 inches (10.2 cm) wide with various lengths, ranging from 2 to 8 inches (5 to 20.3 cm). Sew the pieces together, with the right sides facing, along the 4-inch (10.2 cm) edges to get one long patchwork strip that's 4 x 42 inches (10.2 x 106.7 cm). Press the seam allowances toward one end of the strip.

8 Sew the patchwork strip to the brown rectangles along the 42-inch (106.7 cm) sides. Press the seam allowances toward the brown fabric.

9 Stack and baste the quilt layers together.

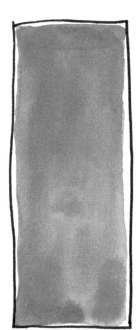

figure 1

10 Mark the center front of the quilt top with a horizontal and vertical chalk line. Using these lines, mark a grid of 2-inch (5 cm) squares. Machine quilt along the lines with brown thread in the needle and gray thread in the bobbin.

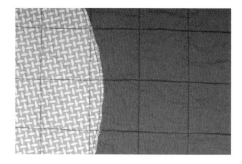

It's a Wrap

11 Bind the quilt with your desired method. Erin cut five 2-inch-wide (5 cm) strips along the aqua fabric's width and used the single-fold binding technique and mitered corners.

Inspire Me!

Looking for even more safari fun? Trade in Skippy, the Elephant, for Spotty, the Giraffe.

Trilogy: River, Morning Glory, and HoJo Space Spores

Flex your embroidery skills with this modern stitched trio. Mix up the size of your stitches by making some thicker and some thinner; simply increase or decrease the number of strands you use.

Victoria Gertenbach

Fabric for Each Quilt

All fabric is cotton, 44 inches (111.8 cm) wide.

QUILT TOP AND BACKING
½ yard (0.5 m) of cream

APPLIQUÉS
¼ yard (0.2 m) each of blue and orange

Notions & Such

Quilting Tool Kit (see page 11)

11 x 8½ inches (27.9 x 21.6 cm) of medium-weight fusible interfacing for each quilt

Pattern transfer materials and tools

¼ yard (0.2 m) of paper-backed fusible webbing, 18 inches (45.7 cm) wide, for each quilt

Low-loft cotton batting

Embroidery needle

Glue stick

9 x 12 inches (22.9 x 30.5 cm) of stiff, heavyweight fusible interfacing for each quilt

6 inches (15.2 cm) of cord for each quilt, for a loop to hang the piece

All-purpose cotton-wrapped sewing thread: blue, cream, and orange

2 skeins each of embroidery floss for the River and Morning Glory quilts*: brown, blue, cream, and orange

4 skeins each of embroidery floss for the HoJo Space Spores quilt*: brown, blue, cream, and orange

*Use 3 or 6 strands when embroidering.

Finished Size of Each Quilt

8 x 11 inches (20.3 x 27.9 cm)—HoJo Space Spores and Morning Glory

11 x 8 inches (27.9 x 20.3 cm)—River

Instructions

These quilts don't have any seam allowances.

Get Scrappy

1 Cut two 11½ x 14-inch pieces (29.2 x 35.6 cm) of the cream-colored fabric for each quilt. Set aside one piece of each pair for the backing. Center and then fuse the medium-weight fusible interfacing on the wrong side of the remaining cream-colored piece in each set, leaving a 1½-inch (3.8 cm) border of fabric around all sides of the interfacing. This is the quilt top background.

Morning Glory

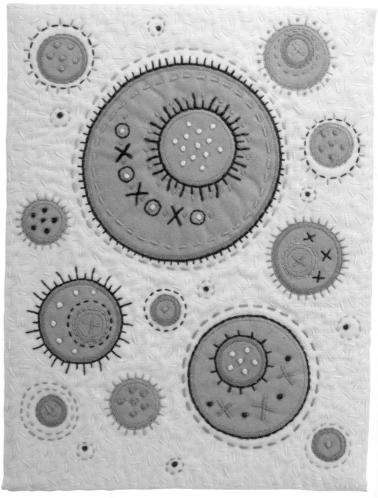

HoJo Space Spores

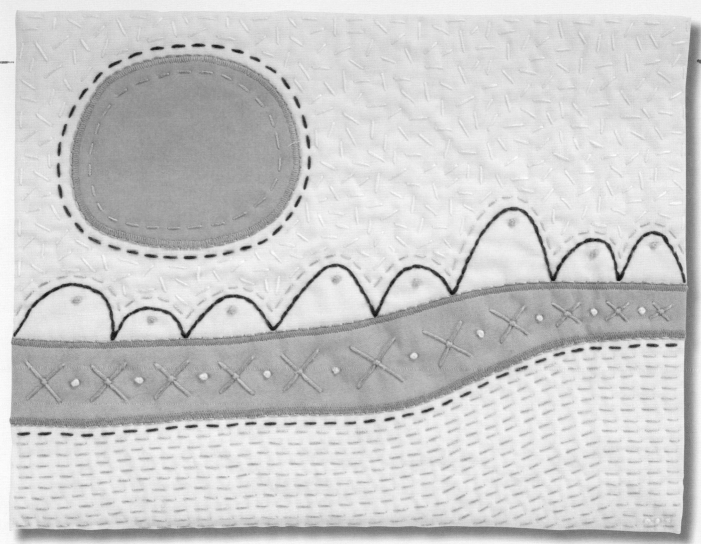

River

Way to Appliqué!

2 Enlarge the whole quilt templates and trace the appliqué shapes onto the paper-backed fusible webbing. Fuse the shapes to the wrong side of the appliqué fabric, and cut them out.

Note: To keep the appliqué edges from fraying, add a ¼-inch (6 mm) border all around when you cut the shapes from the paper-backed fusible webbing. This isn't a seam allowance. Once the webbing is fused to the appliqué fabric, you cut out the shapes without this border.

3 Fuse the appliqués to the right side of the quilt top background, using figures 1, 2, and 3 as a guide. For the Morning Glory quilt, position the bottom of the orange strip along the bottom edge of the cream fabric, and the blue strip so that it overlaps the top of the orange strip ⅛ inch (3 mm).

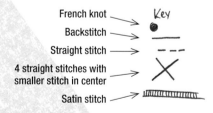

	Key
French knot	●
Backstitch	——
Straight stitch	- - -
4 straight stitches with smaller stitch in center	✕
Satin stitch	⫿⫿⫿⫿⫿

figure 1

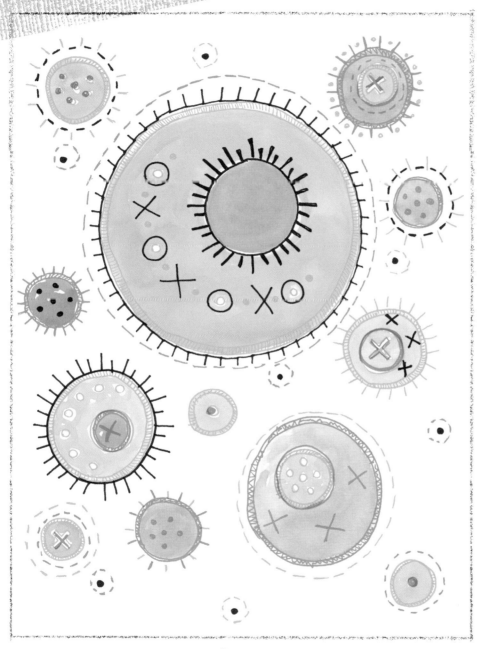

4 Machine stitch around the edges of all of the appliqués, using matching thread and medium-width satin stitches.

5 Cut out an 8½ x 11-inch (21.6 x 27.9 cm) piece of batting for each quilt. Baste the batting to the back of the quilt top.

6 Quilt around the edges of all of the appliqués with matching thread and straight stitches.

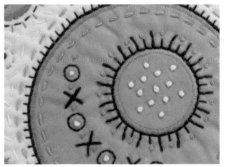

figure 2

Embroider This!

7 Outline the perimeter of the appliqués with backstitches and matching embroidery floss. Referring to the embroidery patterns (see figures 1, 2, and 3), continue embellishing around and inside each shape using the various combinations of the four embroidery colors and a combination of French knots and back, running, and straight stitches.

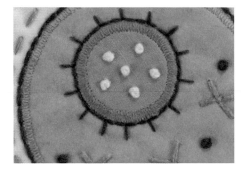

8 Fill in the background with large, randomly spaced straight stitches with the floss colors shown in the embroidery patterns.

It's a Wrap

9 Fold and press the excess cream-colored fabric to the back of each quilt. By doing this, you're wrapping the perimeter of the quilt top

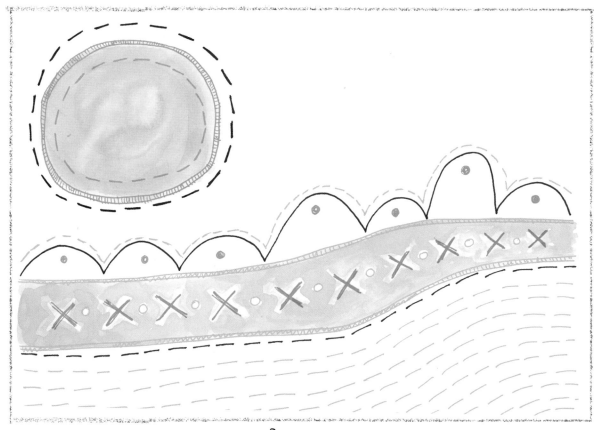

figure 3

around the edges of the batting that's underneath. Dab a glue stick along the underside of the excess fabric to temporarily secure it to the batting.

10 Cut the stiff, heavyweight interfacing ⅛ inch (3 mm) smaller than the prepared top for each quilt. Fuse the interfacing to the center of the wrong side of the backing. Fold and press the sides of the fabric around the back of the interfacing. Use dabs from the glue stick to keep the turned fabric in place.

11 Place the fabric-covered interfacing, fabric side out, on the back of each quilt. Using cream-colored sewing thread, sew

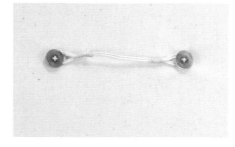

the backing to the top around the perimeter (see figure 4), using appliqué or hidden stitches. The layers are too thick to pin the backing in place before stitching it to the top. Instead, use a dab or two from the glue stick to prevent the backing from shifting. Sew a small cord loop to the center top of each backing for hanging.

Snippet

When embroidering, Victoria prefers to use an embroidery needle with the smallest possible eye. While the large-eyed needles are easier to thread, they are much harder to pull through all the layers of a quilt top and batting. Also, if you have to remove a stitch, a large-eyed needle leaves a larger hole.

figure 4

BEHIND THE SEAMS WITH
xxxxxxxxx xxxxxxxxxx xxxx
Victoria Gertenbach

SEE MORE OF MY STUFF AT: www.sillyboodilly.etsy.com and thesillyboodilly.blogspot.com

MY FIRST BABY WORDS: "Cool man, cool." (Seriously! My mother recorded it in my baby book!)

FAVORITE TUNES TO QUILT TO: The Rolling Stones, Red Hot Chili Peppers, Beck, and Van Morrison.

DESCRIBE YOUR ADDICTION TO FABRIC: All consuming and dangerous.

Giraffes Have Long Necks

Texture adds so much to a quilt; the tactile element is almost as important as how the piece looks, especially when it comes to baby quilts. Free your imagination and consider using nontraditional fabrics and trims such as upholstery yardage and fringe.

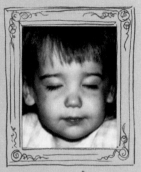

Jude Stuecker

Fabric

All fabric except the giraffe appliqué is 44 inches (111.8 cm) wide.

QUILT TOP
- 1⅓ yards (1.2 m) of mid-weight red upholstery fabric for the background
- 1⅝ yard (1.5 m) mid-weight, bold-print cotton or linen for the border

APPLIQUÉS
- 1¼ yards (1.2 m) of medium- to heavyweight yellow cotton for the giraffe, 36 inches wide (91.4 cm)
- ¼ yard (0.2 m) of fuzzy brown fabric for the spots
- ¼ yard (0.2 m) of green cotton for the letters

BACKING
- 1⅓ yards (1.2 m) of a blue, white, and light brown print

BINDING
- ¼ yard (0.2 m) of dark brown

Notions & Such

Quilting Tool Kit (see page 11)

Appliqué pattern (page 134)

Pattern transfer materials and tools

2 yards (1.8 m) of paper-backed fusible webbing, 22 inches (55.9 cm) wide

⅔ yard (0.6 m) of gold drapery fringe for the giraffe's mane, 1½ inches (3.8 cm) wide

2-inch (5 cm) square each of felt for the eye: black and white

Medium-loft cotton batting

Embroidery needle

All-purpose polyester sewing thread: brown, gold, and green

Skein each of embroidery floss: brown and gold

Finished Size

44 x 54 inches (111.8 x 137.2 cm)

115

Instructions

All of the seam allowances are ¼ inch (6 mm) wide.

Get Scrappy

1 Cut the quilt top background fabric to 36½ x 46½ inches (92.7 x 118.1 cm). If you're willing to cut the strips on the crosswise grain and piece the longer strips, you only need ⅔ yard (0.6 m) for the borders.

𝒩ote: If your background fabric isn't heavy enough to support the appliqués, apply mid- or heavyweight fusible interfacing to the back. Upholstery fabric won't need it, but cotton will. When in doubt, it's always better to use it. You'll need 1⅜ yards (1.3 m).

Way to Appliqué!

2 Enlarge the appliqué patterns, flip them over, and trace them onto the paper side of the paper-backed fusible webbing. Fuse the shapes to the wrong side of the appliqué fabric, and cut them out. Transfer the placement marks for the spots, nose, and eye.

3 Place the giraffe on the background (look at the finished quilt photo as a guide), tuck the mane trim under the left side of the neck, and iron down the giraffe. You might need to pin the trim's header to the background.

4 Thread your sewing machine with the gold thread, and select a zigzag stitch with a wide width and short length. Sew around the edges of the giraffe, catching the fringe in the stitching as you work along the neck.

Snippet

5 Fuse the brown appliqué spots and nose onto the giraffe, and sew them in place with the brown thread and the same stitch. Sew on the eye circles, one at a time, using the matching thread and with the black felt positioned on top of the white.

𝒩ote: Although it's easier to attach the spots and eyes to the giraffe before the body is applied to the quilt top, by adding them after the body is sewn to the top, you're creating a longer-lasting piece. One line of stitches around the edges of a body this big is probably not very stable in the long run, especially if the quilt is going to get washed a lot.

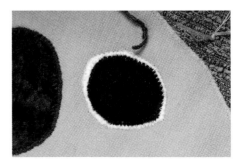

6 Appliqué the letters to the quilt top.

Sew It Up

7 Cut two strips from the border fabric that are 4½ x 36½ inches (11.4 x 92.7 cm). Sew these to the top and bottom edges of the quilt top. Cut off the excess fabric. Cut the side borders to the same width but 54½ inches (138.4 cm) long. Sew them to the top. Press the seam allowances toward the center of the quilt.

8 Stack the quilt layers. Tie them together with the embroidery floss (without separating the strands), using brown on the giraffe and gold on the background.

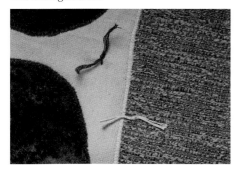

It's a Wrap

9 Bind the quilt with your desired method. Jude cut 1¼-inch-wide (3.2 cm) strips along the fabric length and used the single-fold binding technique.

Snippet
If you lighten the pressure of the presser foot, you'll find it easier to turn corners when stitching appliqués to the quilt top.

BEHIND THE SEAMS WITH

x x x x x x x x x x x x x x x x x
Jude Stuecker

SEE MORE OF MY STUFF AT: www.judestuecker.com

MOST TREASURED BABY BLANKET: Actually a baby diaper that I carried around and sniffed constantly.

TACKIEST THING I EVER MADE: A dress out of a Star Wars bed sheet.

WHEN I FINISH A QUILT, I FEEL LIKE: Going to the chiropractor.

Little Crosses

This is a great first patchwork project: crosses that are a little crooked add to the quirky charm of the quilt. Use a dark color for the background to create a fun, bold quilt, or make all of the crosses out of the same fabric for a minimalist effect.

Marné Cales

Fabrics

All fabric is cotton, 44 inches (111.8 cm) wide.

QUILT TOP
1¼ yards (1.1 m) of white
¼ yard (0.2 m) each of 6 medium- and small-scale cotton prints

QUILT BACKING
1⅜ yards (1.2 m) of coordinating small-scale floral print

BINDING
⅜ yard (0.3 m) of small-scale blue floral print

Notions & Such

Quilting Tool Kit (see page 11)

Low-loft cotton batting

All-purpose cotton-wrapped white sewing thread

Bright turquoise cotton quilting thread

Finished Size

32 x 44 inches (81.3 x 111.8 cm)

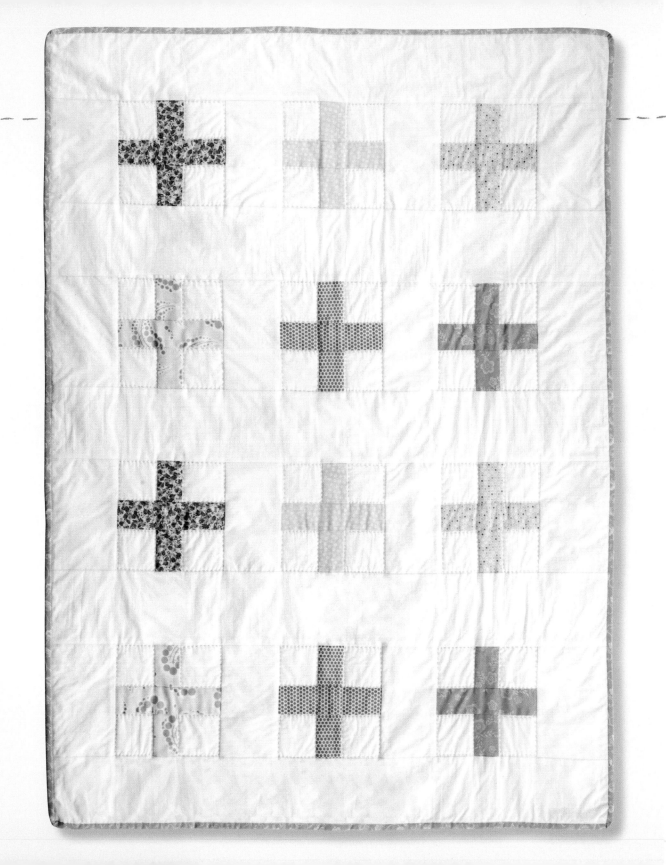

Cutting Chart for White Background Fabric

	Quantity	Width	Height
A	48	2¾" (7 cm)	2¾" (7 cm)
B	8	3½" (8.9 cm)	6½" (16.5 cm)
C	8	4½" (11.4 cm)	6½" (16.5 cm)
D	5	36½" (92.7 cm)	4½" (11.4 cm)

Cutting Chart for Print Cross Fabrics

	Quantity	Width	Height
E	24	2¾" (7 cm)	2" (5 cm)
F	12	6½" (16.5 cm)	2" (5 cm)

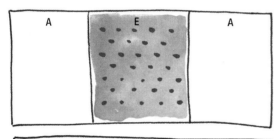
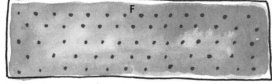
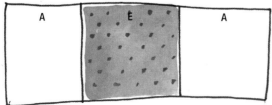

figure 1

Instructions

All of the seam allowances are ¼ inch (6 mm) wide unless otherwise noted.

Get Scrappy

1   Cut the fabrics for the quilt top as detailed in the cutting charts.

Building Blocks

2   Use the white thread to piece the entire quilt top on your sewing machine, and refer to figure 1 for the block assembly: Sew a white square A to both long sides of a print rectangle E. Sew this pieced strip to a print rectangle F. Press all of the seams toward the middle. Make another A-E-A pieced strip, and sew it to the opposite edge of the same rectangle F. Make 11 more blocks, for a total of two of each quilt top print.

3   Refer to figure 2 to join pieces to make a row: Sew a white rectangle B between two blocks. Attach another white rectangle B and then another block. Sew a white rectangle C to both ends of this pieced strip. Press the seam allowances away from each block. This completes one row. Make four rows.

Sew It Up

4 Sew the rows together, with a white strip D between each pieced row. Again, press all of the seam allowances away from the blocks.

5 Stack and baste the quilt layers together.

6 Quilt small squares just inside the seams in each white square A, using the turquoise quilting thread.

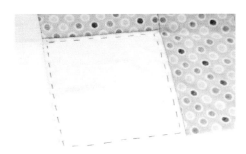

It's a Wrap

7 Bind the quilt with your desired method. Marné cut five 2-inch-wide (5 cm) strips and used the double-layer binding technique.

BEHIND THE SEAMS WITH
× × × × × × × × × × × × × × × × × ×
Marné Cales

SEE MORE STUFF AT: http://www.heylucy.net/

LEAST FAVORITE CHILDHOOD NICKNAME: Moose—I was always taller than the boys.

WHEN I GROW UP: I want to be an exotic animal trainer or a forest ranger.

FIRST SEWING PROJECT: A little purse I made from scraps of fabric leftover from my mom's occupation at the time: sewing high-tech backpacking tents. I sewed the whole thing by hand from rip-stop nylon.

Snippet
You can use fat quarters (see page 9) for the cotton prints for the blocks, rather than yardage.

C | B | B | C

figure 2

All Lined Up

The traditional log cabin design goes bold and modern thanks to the scale of the blocks and the organic feel of the stripes. Freehand stripes lead to lovely imperfections that give this quilt its jazzy flavor.

Malka Dubrawsky

Fabric

All fabric is cotton, 44 inches (111.8 cm) wide.

QUILT TOP
- ¼ yard (0.3 m) of each of the following colors: burnt orange, citrus yellow, dark pink, dark red, pale orange, raspberry, rust brown, and sand
- ½ yard (0.5 m) of each of the following colors: blue, dark green, light green, mustard, orange, pale pink, pale yellow, purple, red, turquoise, and yellow

QUILT BACKING
3 yards (2.7 m) of orange

Notions & Such

Quilting Tool Kit (see page 11)

Low-loft cotton batting

All-purpose cotton-wrapped, neutral-colored sewing thread

Turquoise quilting thread

9 sealable plastic sandwich bags

Finished Size

48 inches (121.9 cm) square

Strip Color Combinations Chart

Dark green	Light green
Dark pink	Raspberry
	Pale pink
	Purple
Orange	Yellow
Pale orange	Dark red
	Rust brown
Red	Citrus yellow
	Mustard
	Orange
Sand	Burnt orange
Turquoise	Blue
	Mustard
	Purple
	Yellow

Instructions

All of the seam allowances are ¼ inch (6 mm) wide.

Get Scrappy

1 Cut all the quilt top fabric into strips that range from 1½ to 2 inches (3.8 to 5 cm) wide and are as long as the entire length of the fabric. Use a rotary cutter and self-healing mat to cut these strips, but work without a ruler so that the cuts aren't perfect.

2 Using the color combination chart, sew strips together along their lengths (figure 1). Note that some colors are paired up in more than one combination. Use your template pieces to get a sense of how much of any given combination you need to create the blocks. After making any seams, always press both seam allowances to the side with the darker fabric.

Building Blocks

3 Enlarge the whole quilt template (figure 2) , and cut it apart to make templates (patterns) for all of the smaller squares and rectangles that make up the entire quilt top. Make sure that you can read the number and color combination on each template before you cut them out. Place the templates for each block into a separate sandwich bag. Write the block number on the bag.

4 Cut out the fabric pieces for block 1 using the bagged templates and striped fabric you created. Add a seam allowance to every edge as you cut out each fabric piece.

figure 1

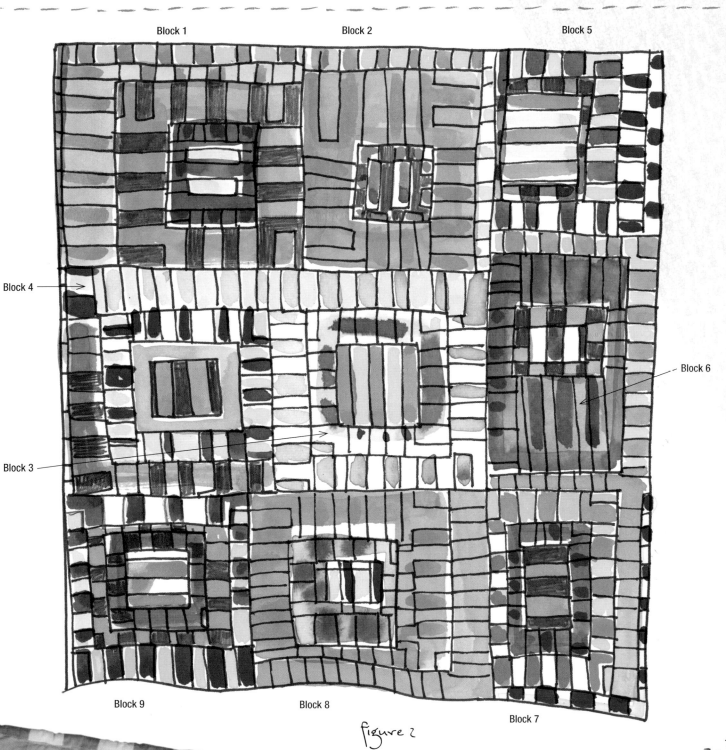

Block 1   Block 2   Block 5

Block 4

Block 6

Block 3

Block 9   Block 8

Block 7

figure 2

5 Refer to figure 2, and sew together the pieces for block 1, starting with the center square and adding a piece (fabric strip) at a time. Continue adding pieces until the block is complete. Assemble the remaining blocks in the same fashion.

Tip: The order that the strips are added is best left to improvisation. Just look for a strip that's the same length as one of the sides of the growing block.

Sew It Up

6 Sew block 1 to block 2 and block 3 to block 4. Sew these two pairs to each other along the long edge to create a four patch. Then sew block 5 to block 6 and then attach this to the four patch. Sew blocks 7, 8, and 9 together, and add this row of blocks to the remainder of the quilt top.

7 Stack the quilt layers on a flat surface. Following the quick turn method (page 28), place the batting down first, then the backing (with the right side up), and then the quilt top (with the right side facing down).

8 Baste the three layers together. Sew around the perimeter, leaving an 18-inch (45.7 cm) opening for turning.

9 Trim the backing and batting to the same size as the quilt top. Remove the basting, and turn the quilt right side out. Hand-stitch the opening closed.

10 Baste the quilt top and then hand or machine quilt through all of the layers along the seam lines.

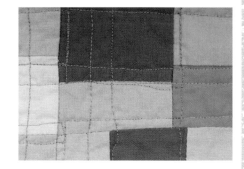

BEHIND THE SEAMS WITH
xxxxxxxxxxxxxxxxxxxxxxxxxxxx
Malka Dubrawsky

SEE MORE OF MY STUFF AT: stitchindye.blogspot.com or www.flickr.com/photos/stitchindye/ or stitchindye.etsy.com

ONE WORD THAT BEST DESCRIBES YOUR ARTISTIC STYLE: Improvised.

DESCRIBE YOUR ADDICTION TO FABRIC: I can quit anytime I want. Isn't that what all addicts say?

FAVORITE TUNES TO QUILT TO: I don't like music when I'm sewing; it's too distracting. But I love listening to NPR.

I Heart Plushy

Christina Romeo

Who can resist a starry-eyed plushy? Using a large-scale appliqué, the quick-turn binding method, and machine satin stitching for the quilting, you can create this quilt in just a few hours. The back side is made with a single expanse of blissfully soft fleece.

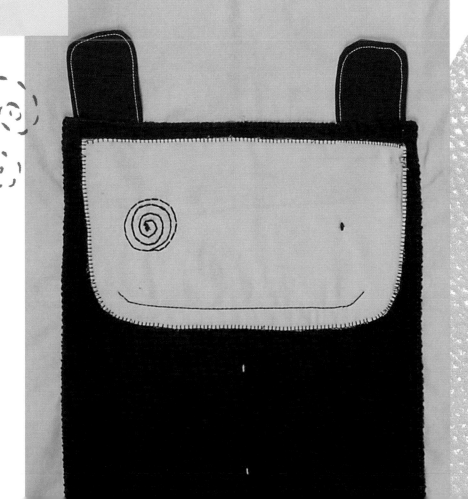

Instructions

All of the seam allowances are ¼ inch (6 mm) wide unless otherwise noted.

Get Scrappy

1 Cut the quilt top background fabric to 34½ x 45 inches (87.6 x 114.3 cm).

2 For the appliqué, cut the corduroy to 10½ x 19 inches (26.7 x 48.3 cm), the brown cotton into four 2 x 3½-inch (5 x 8.9 cm) ear pieces and two 2½ x 6-inch (6.4 x 15.2 cm) leg pieces, and the light yellow cotton to 9 x 5 inches (22.9 x 12.7 cm). Cut the red print fabric into two rough heart shapes.

3 Round the bottom corners of the light yellow piece and the bottom edge of the two leg pieces.

Way to Appliqué!

4 To make the ears, pin two ear pieces together with right sides facing. Stitch a curved line to create the top curved edge of the ear. Clip the corners, turn the shape inside out, and topstitch around the edge with white thread. Complete the other ear in the same way.

5 Machine stitch around the inside edge of both leg pieces with white thread.

Fabrics

All fabric is 44 inches (111.8 cm) wide.

QUILT TOP
   1¼ yards (1.1 m) of yellow cotton

APPLIQUÉS
   ¼ yard (0.2 m) of red print cotton for the hearts
   ¼ yard (0.2 m) of brown cotton for the ears and legs
   ¼ yard (0.2 m) of light yellow cotton for the face
   ¼ yard (0.2 m) of brown corduroy for the body

QUILT BACKING
   1¼ yards (1.1 m) of white fleece

Notions & Such

Quilting Tool Kit (see page 11)

Low-loft cotton batting

All-purpose cotton-wrapped white, yellow, and brown sewing thread

Brown and white embroidery thread

Finished Size

34 x 44½ inches (86.4 x 113 cm)

6   Pin the light yellow face piece to the corduroy rectangle. Blanket-stitch—using your machine or by hand—around the edge. Use a satin stitch to create one eye and a running stitch to create the smile. Using the brown embroidery thread, hand stitch the spiral for the other eye with running stitches.

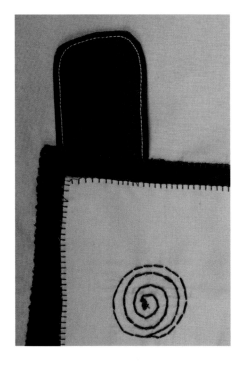

7   Pin the legs to the quilt top, using the photo as a guide. Blanket-stitch around the edge of each leg.

8   Press under the edges of the corduroy piece ¼ inch (6 mm), and pin it in place over the legs on the quilt top. Tuck the ears under the top edge of the body, leaving the tops free. Stitch around the entire body shape.

9   Use white embroidery thread and running stitches to create the two stitched heart shapes above the bear.

10   Press under the edges of the red print heart shapes. Pin them to the quilt, and machine stitch around the edges with white thread.

Sew It Up

11   Following the quick-turn method (page 28), place the backing faceup on top of the batting and center the quilt top facedown on top. Pin and sew around the edge, using a ½-inch (1.3 cm) seam allowance and leaving a 10-inch (25.4 cm) opening at the bottom. Cut off the excess batting and backing, and trim across the corners.

12   Turn the quilt right side out. Topstitch around the entire outside edge using a ¼-inch (6 mm) seam allowance, making sure you stitch the opening closed.

13   Load your sewing machine with yellow thread and the bobbin with white thread. Use a satin stitch to create ties around your quilt, including three in the center of the bear body.

Inspire Me!

You've got lots of options when it comes to cute plushy creatures; check out this engaging trio.

BEHIND THE SEAMS WITH

Christina Romeo

SEE MORE OF MY STUFF AT: http://jamtartbaby.etsy.com

SEWING IDOL: Hands down...Denyse Schmidt.

WHEN I FINISH A QUILT: I feel relieved and happy although it's always short-lived; I know there's another project staring at me from the corner screaming "finish me," "finish me!"

MOST CHALLENGING THING ABOUT QUILTING: Time management. When I start a quilt, I don't want to stop, but then there are those children that live in my house, and they always want to get fed and stuff.

Quilt Templates

Enlarge templates to dimensions or desired size. Some templates may need to be reversed, depending on your technique.

Monkey Business

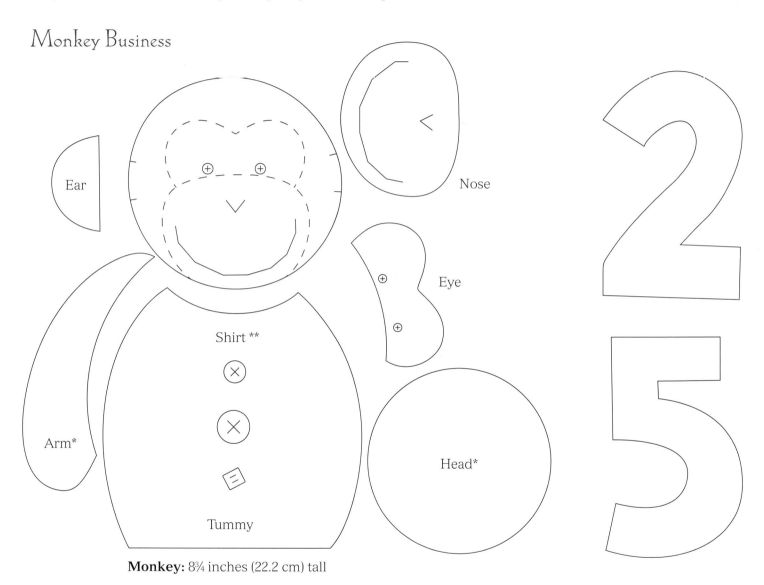

Ear

Nose

Eye

Shirt **

Arm*

Tummy

Head*

Monkey: 8¾ inches (22.2 cm) tall

Add ¼-inch (6 mm) seam allowance unless otherwise noted.
* Allowance is included.
** Allowance is included for shirtless monkey.

Monkey Business

Numerals: 4½ inches (11.4 cm) tall

Flowers: 5 inches (12.7 cm) across
Banana: 6½ inches (16.5 cm) tall
Largest circle: 4¾ inches (12 cm) in diameter

Quilt Templates

Enlarge templates to dimensions or desired size. Some templates may need to be reversed, depending on your technique.

Giraffes Have Long Necks

GIRAFFES HAVE LONG NECKS.

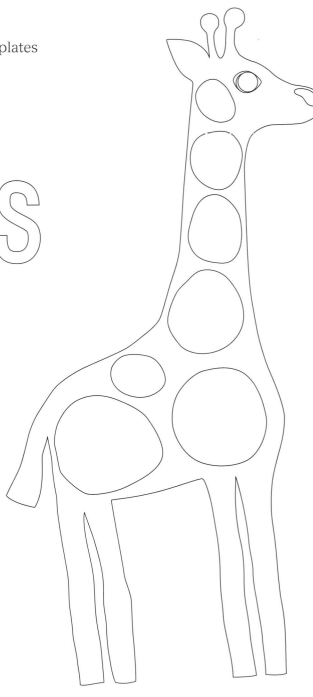

Letters: 4 inches (10.2 cm) tall
Giraffe: 47½ inches (120.7 cm) tall

Stair-Crazy

Kitties: 4 inches (10.2 cm) tall

135

Quilt Templates

Enlarge templates to dimensions or desired size. Some templates may need to be reversed, depending on your technique.

Good Night, Moon, Good Morning, Sun

GOOD
MORNING

GOOD
NIGHT

Birds: 31 inches (78.7 cm) tall
Sun: 11½ inches (29.2 cm) in diameter

Cloud: 11 inches (27.9 cm) across
Letters: 4 inches (10.2 cm) tall

Branch: 30 inches (76.2 cm) long
Stars: 3¾ inches (9.5 cm) across

Over the Orchard

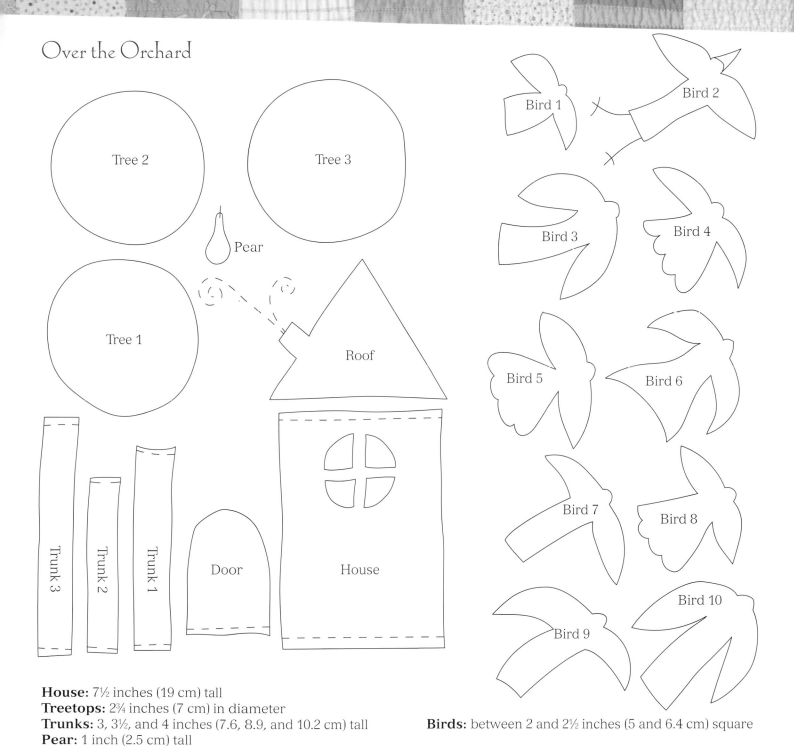

Tree 2

Tree 3

Pear

Tree 1

Roof

Trunk 3

Trunk 2

Trunk 1

Door

House

Bird 1

Bird 2

Bird 3

Bird 4

Bird 5

Bird 6

Bird 7

Bird 8

Bird 9

Bird 10

House: 7½ inches (19 cm) tall
Treetops: 2¾ inches (7 cm) in diameter
Trunks: 3, 3½, and 4 inches (7.6, 8.9, and 10.2 cm) tall
Pear: 1 inch (2.5 cm) tall

Birds: between 2 and 2½ inches (5 and 6.4 cm) square

Quilt Templates

Enlarge templates to dimensions or desired size. Some templates may need to be reversed, depending on your technique.

Skippy, the Elephant

Elephant: 38 inches (96.5 cm) wide

Giddyup, Sea Horse

Sea horse: 13½ inches (34.3 cm) tall

Woodland Creatures

Patterns are 75% of actual size.

Red Shoe Dog

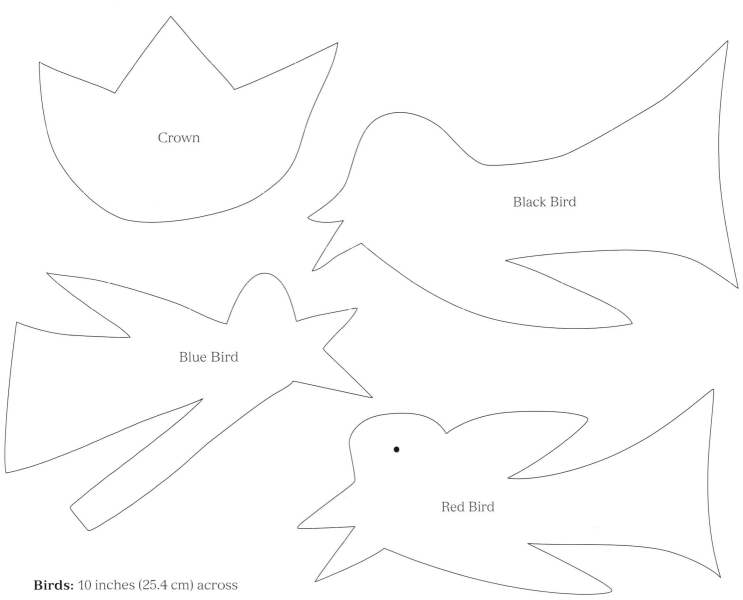

Crown

Black Bird

Blue Bird

Red Bird

Birds: 10 inches (25.4 cm) across

Quilt Templates

Enlarge templates to dimensions or desired size. Some templates
may need to be reversed, depending on your technique.

Red Shoe Dog

Background Templates
Enlarge to listed dimensions.

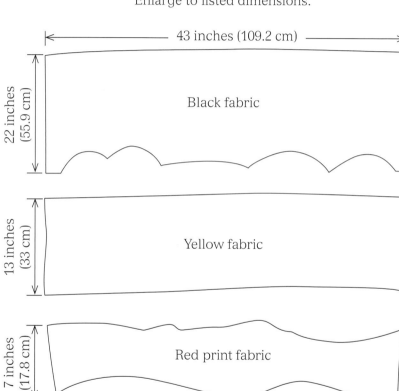

43 inches (109.2 cm)

22 inches (55.9 cm)

Black fabric

13 inches (33 cm)

Yellow fabric

7 inches (17.8 cm)

Red print fabric

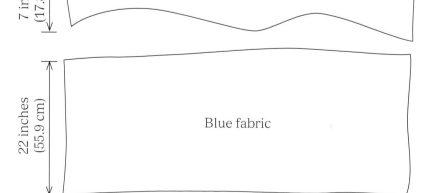

22 inches (55.9 cm)

Blue fabric

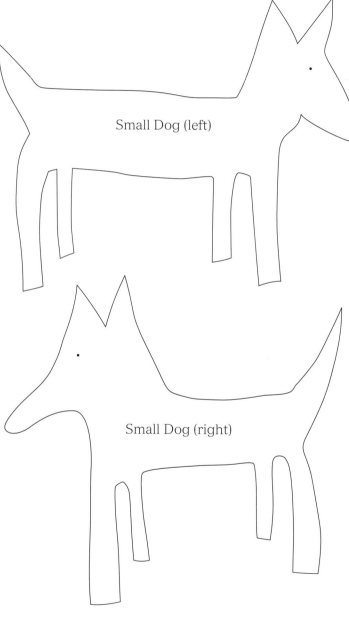

Small Dog (left)

Small Dog (right)

Small dogs: 7 inches (17.8 cm) tall

Red Shoe Dog

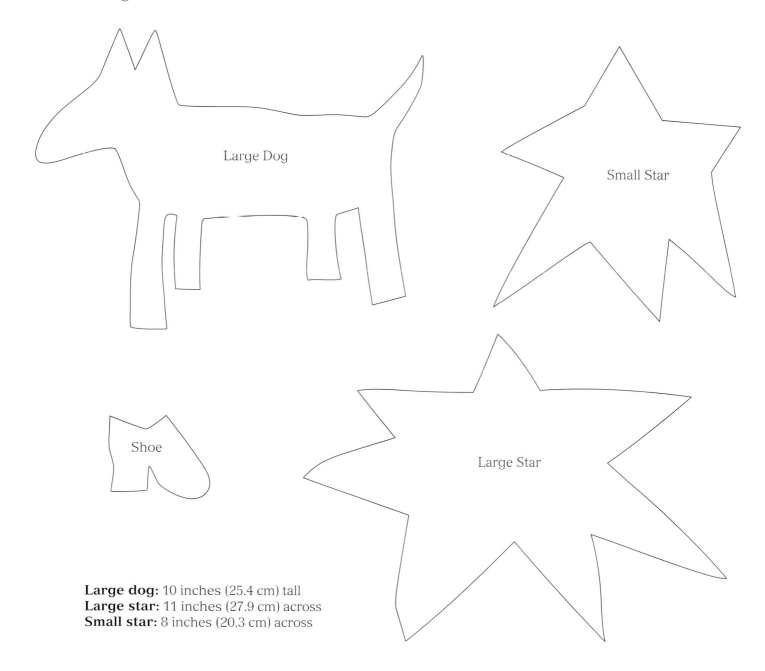

Large Dog

Small Star

Shoe

Large Star

Large dog: 10 inches (25.4 cm) tall
Large star: 11 inches (27.9 cm) across
Small star: 8 inches (20.3 cm) across

About the Designers

Benares Angeley

Benares Angeley was born in a cabin her parents built in the mountains of Virginia and now lives in New Bedford, Massachusetts. She grew up sleeping under a quilt made by her great-grandmother and inherited the sewing machine she uses to this day from her mother. At age ten, she made her first outfit—a hot pink miniskirt—and has since then seen a needle and thread as two of her greatest allies in life. When she's not sewing, she can be found playing accordion, banjo, or guitar with her husband.

Marné Cales

Marné Cales has loved making things since the age of six, when she created a tiny purse from scraps of nylon. Barbie clothes soon followed. She watched her mother and grandmother quilt but had no interest in the craft until she was a teenager and decided to teach herself how to do it with the aid of a library book. She studied clothing and textiles in college, and her love of textiles continued to grow over the years. A technical writer by day, Marné cuddles up with one or more of her two cats and two dogs at night and creates everything from sweaters to quilts. She documents her creative life on her blog www.heylucy.net.

Glynis Cotton

Glynis Cotton made her first quilt for her college senior art show. She used an iron on/photocopy method to superimpose images of herself wearing vintage girdles onto the girdles themselves. She then sewed the girdles onto a rectangular piece of upholstery, sandwiched it with batting and backing fabric, and hung it on the wall. It was a mess and she had no idea what she was doing, but even then she was drawn to the idea of quilting. Glynis loves the

history of women's hands that quilting holds. She finds it interesting that she can attach bits and pieces together and alchemically create something completely new.

Malka Dubrawsky

Malka Dubrawsky grew up watching her mother sew and knit and was introduced to art in Mrs. Stapleton's eighth grade art class. And she hasn't been the same since. Malka went on to graduate from college with a BFA in Studio Art, though at the time she was primarily making prints and drawing. Being at home with children inspired her to work with textiles, eventually leading to various explorations with dyeing and patterning fabric. More recently, Malka has been interested in making more functional textiles, primarily out of her hand-dyed and patterned fabric. To this end, she has turned her attention to crafting quilts, pillows, and other sundries for sale via her online store, http://stitchindye.etsy.com.

Laura Ducommun

Laura Ducommun has been quilting and designing for almost 12 years. It wasn't until she saw a television show profiling modern quilts that she really understood the connection between modern design and the art of hand quilting. She found that quilts did not have to be old fashioned; they could be exciting, modern, and fresh. Laura loves to create quilts with fun designs that have a modern edge and sells many of her quilts locally and online. She was also featured at one of The W Hotel and *Dwell* Magazine's silent auctions to raise money for Hurricane Katrina relief.

Victoria Gertenbach

Victoria Gertenbach has loved fabric and thread since she was a very young girl and continually delights in exploring its endless possibilities. Her work has appeared in Somerset Studio and many sister publications, along with the books *Material Visions* and *Transparent Art* (Stampington & Co. 2004 and 2005) as well as the *Collage, Artplay for Your Creative Spirit 2009* wall calendar (Amber Lotus). She lives in Lancaster, Pennsylvania, with her husband and children. Visit her blog at http://thesillyboodilly.blogspot.com.

Erin Harris

Erin Harris is a stay-at-home mom to two young girls. As a young child, she was always making things, including many woven potholders and plastic canvas embroideries. Erin learned to sew in home ec while in junior high and thinks it was the best class she ever took. She knits, crochets, and embroiders, but sewing is her real love. These days, Erin has a few projects going at all times and finds time to craft between chasing children and driving carpools. Follow Erin's adventures in craft at her website, www.houseonhillroad.com.

Julie Knoblock

Julie Knoblock lives in Victoria, Australia, with her partner Jim and her two dogs, Bender and Leela. Julie has achieved success through professional illustrating, though these days she usually spends her time creating quirky and unique art, prints, and handmade items for her own label Tummy Ache. Julie found making a baby quilt for this book especially pleasing. While she was making it, she discovered she was pregnant with her first baby.

Aimee Ray

Aimee Ray has been making things for as long as she can remember, and she has a head full of ideas. As a graphic designer in the greeting card and comic book industries—and with several personal projects in the works—she is never without something creative in hand. Her interests range from digital painting and illustration to sewing stuffed animals, embroidery, and everything else in between. She is the author of *Doodle Stitching* (Lark, 2007), a book of contemporary embroidery designs and projects. You can see more of Aimee's work at her website, www.dreamfollow.com.

Christina Romeo

Growing up in a family of left brainers, Christina Romeo was viewed as the "quirky" child, the one constantly tearing apart pillows, clothing, and just about anything to reconstruct into fashionable attire and creepy dolls. She was very lucky at an early age to spend time with a "grandmotherly" caregiver who taught her the fine art of the stitch and creating handmade works, a common thread throughout her life. Born and raised in the United States, Christina now resides in beautiful British Columbia, Canada, working as a mixed-media artist combining stitch and her passion for painting to create works on canvas and cloth.

Dorie Blaisdell Schwarz

Dorie Blaisdell Schwarz is a living antidote to Jersey girl stereotypes. While she does have a fondness for great shoes, Dorie also loves old houses and other random, worn, and long-forgotten things. Old memories actually inspire many of her designs, whether they're created on a sewing machine, with knitting needles, as a screen print, or with a glue gun. New Jersey still has a big soft spot in her heart, but Dorie currently lives in a small town called Farmer City, Illinois, with her husband and their young daughter. When she's not sewing or crafting, she's building websites and "helping" renovate her Victorian-era farmhouse. She keeps a craft blog at tumblingblocks.net/blog.

Carly Schwerdt

Carly Schwerdt lives in Adelaide, Australia, with her two adorable little girls, Lily and Olive, and her super husband Chris. She runs an art studio for children, called Nest Studio, that has a sweet little boutique attached. Carly loves to support other independent artists and designers by selling their wares as well as other unique gifts from Japan and Europe. Carly is a graphic designer and qualified primary school teacher who, in her spare time, designs textiles for her other business, Umbrella Prints, co-owned with fellow artist Amy Prior. Visit her websites at www.neststudio.typepad.com and www.umbrellaprints.typepad.com.

Jude Stuecker

When Jude Stuecker's grandmother bought her an old sewing machine at the age of 14, Jude knew she was in for some good times. A couple of years later, she made her first art quilt from a photograph of her sister's face—a daunting, yet inspiring project. Sixteen years later, she's still cranking them out. Originally from Louisville, Kentucky, she now lives and works in her home in Asheville, North Carolina, with her husband, stepson, and five cats.

Kajsa Wikman

Born in Finland, Kajsa Wikman specialized in paper cutting at the age of five, much to the chagrin of her parents. As a teenager, Kajsa accompanied her mother to a quilting class and has been hooked ever since. She attended her first craft fair soon after receiving her Masters in Ethnology and having her first child, Elsa. Kajsa has just recently started her own business, Syko Design, to become a fulltime designer and crafter.

Laurraine Yuyama

Laurraine Yuyama used to work as a custom picture framer but found herself wanting to create her own art instead. She now spends her days surrounded with beautiful fabric, buttons, ribbons, and clay. In the last five years, she has developed a style of surface design that she uses with both pottery and quilted items, combining beautiful patterns from nature with unique functional items such as bags and bowls. Laurraine is a self-taught quilter, and she creates all of her own designs and patterns. She takes inspiration from new fabric, buttons, Japanese craft books, and the Internet craft community. When she's not crafting, she spends time with her little girl and her husband. Her work is sold internationally from her home-based studio in Vancouver, Canada, and through her online shop, which you can find at www.patchworkpottery.com.

Index